KYLENE BEERS & ROBE

FORGED BY READING

THE POWER OF A LITERATE LIFE

SCHOLASTIC

Forged by Reading
**is dedicated to an unsung genius, silversmith,
and creator of the Cherokee syllabary,**

Sequoyah
ᏍᏏᏉᏯᎢ

Sequoyah (c. 1770–1843), a Cherokee, spent his early life as a silversmith and blacksmith, forging beautiful work with his silver patterns. As an adult, though, he became enamored with what he called "talking leaves," the writing he saw from white settlers. He recognized that these "talking leaves" allowed the white people to communicate with one another in a way the Cherokees—or other First Nations people—could not, for at this time there was no written language for any of the First Nations people. He wanted his people to have this power of communication and independence.

Sequoyah made it his life's work to change that. He began creating a written Cherokee language in 1809. By 1821 he had created an 86-symbol syllabary, something never before done by anyone who was not literate in any language. By 1825, his syllabary became the official written language of the Cherokee nation. Soon, the literacy rate of the Cherokees surpassed that of white settlers.

After the United States Congress passed the Indian Removal Act of 1830, Cherokees were forced to migrate along what is now called the Trail of Tears. Though they could take few belongings, they could take what would forever be theirs as a result of Sequoyah: the ability to read and write.

His forging fires helped him mold silver into intricate patterns; and the fire of his mind helped him bring reading and writing to his great Cherokee nation and then many other First Nations people.

We chose this portrait of Sequoyah by Daniel HorseChief because the quill and paper he holds represent his contribution to literacy. HorseChief, a Cherokee/Pawnee award-winning artist and sculptor, is known for his work that portrays historic and contemporary Native American themes. We are grateful for HorseChief's willingness to share his art with us.

Contents

Part III: Hope

66 I feel that we have a very naive political philosophy, in terms of human rights. . . . In order for a democracy to work, those who have the most sometimes have to give up more. It's like playing in a jazz band. You can't stand up and solo all night yourself, even if you're the best soloist. You have to play the background sometimes, and let someone else develop and play.

. . . Because everyone is playing, and you're trying to make them sound good, and they're trying to make you sound good, and you're inventing what you're playing at the moment that you're playing it. So there's a lot going on. It's an actual representation of what goes on. It's a musical representation of what goes on in a working democracy. You have to want to play with other people to play jazz music. You can't just play your part. 'Cause your part is their part.

. . . But if you were concerned for human rights, the first things you would address are human rights in your own country. The striving for dignity and freedom lies within the hearts of all people. No government can take that from people. 99

Wynton Marsalis
Musician, Composer, Writer, Speaker, Activist

INTRODUCTION

We Turn to You

TODAY, DEAR TEACHERS, AS WITH EACH TODAY, we turn to you. We have said before, and now say again louder and with more conviction, as teachers we proudly stand beside you, but as parents we stand in awe of all that you do. On behalf of a grateful nation, thank you. You withstand the fires of uncertainty, of fear, of inequities. You show the nation that teachers always respond to their students no matter the situation. Thank you.

We published *Disrupting Thinking: Why* How *We Read Matters* in 2017, which meant we were writing it in 2016 and thinking about it in 2014–2015. We're slow thinkers. Or thorough. We prefer *thorough,* though our editors might lean more toward *slow.*

The point is, those years of thinking and writing now seem like ages ago. We had no idea all the disruptions we would each face since the publication of that book. With all of the changes that have happened in our world, we have no crystal ball that lets us predict what will happen next. What we can do, though, is connect some dots and share them now with you in *Forged by Reading*. Perhaps these connections will help you in these next months and years as you think about your curricular choices, about the books your students will read, about the reading and writing choices you put before them, about the strategies you choose to share, about the language you choose to use, and the personal biases you choose to examine. Perhaps this book will help you help even one child find his or her way to what we hope will be a better tomorrow.

This book you hold is a culmination of our life's work as professional educators who have taught in public schools and universities, served on national boards, and held national positions. We've been consultants to the National Governors Association, won awards, beamed[1] with pride when our books received accolades, but always felt the most fulfilled when teachers told us that something we had written had helped them rethink something they were doing, had made a difference in their students' literate lives. Those days, we could say to each other that all the work had been worth it, because it helped one teacher help one kid.

66 That's what you do, teachers. You help kids. 99

That's what you do, teachers. You help kids. You help them become the best version of themselves, one that they might not even see and that you only glimpse. We need you to keep doing that because our problems are only going to grow more complex—that we do know.

So, in this book, we take a slight detour from what many of our previous books have done. Rather than adding more strategies to the already overcrowded world of reading strategies, we instead delve deeper into issues we think must be confronted and solved, *finally*. Or, if not solved, at least put on the agenda so they are addressed. Does that mean we no longer support valuable reading strategies? Of course not. It just means that if you've learned our Three Big Questions (presented in *Reading Nonfiction: Stances, Signposts, and*

---

[1] Kylene beamed. I don't beam. *-rep*

Strategies, 2015), then you don't have to worry that here we have morphed them into Three Hundred Big Questions. And the Signposts (first introduced in *Notice and Note: Strategies for Close Reading,* 2013) have not turned into an atlas book of directions.

What this book does do is go back to what we probably have never said loudly enough, long enough, bravely enough, or adamantly enough. This book is about the power of a literate life because it explains that literacy is not just about reading and writing. Reading and writing are the *tools* of literacy. But literacy is power. Literacy is privilege. And in this country, that power and privilege have been kept the purview of white people. In fact, for the Black, Indigenous, and People of Color (BIPOC), the history of literacy has been the history of the suppression of literacy, the suppression of power. We'll return to these ideas throughout this book, but we wanted you to know up front that we're offering ideas here that are bigger than arguing over the Lexile level of a book. We're not addressing whether classroom libraries should be leveled or the difference between a strategy and a skill. We've done those things in our previous books, and we think they are worth discussing—some other time.

> **❝Now, right now, our discussion as a nation needs to be about how reading and writing offer students the power to change themselves and perhaps the world around them.❞**

Now, right now, our discussion as a nation needs to be about how reading and writing offer students the power to change themselves and perhaps the world around them. We will never have all the money we want to pay teachers what they ought to be paid, to build schools that foster intellectual communities. But we can pause to remember why we teach literature, teach reading: to remind young people that no matter how hard life might become, no matter how many things try to shape them into something else, they can be shaped—forged— by reading.

So, join us on this journey. We know if we will have a better tomorrow, it will be in large part because of you. So, once again, dear teachers, we turn to you.

Please see the companion website at scholastic.com/BeersandProbstFBR for videos and additional resources.

PART I

Change

Never doubt that a small group of thoughtful,
committed citizens can change the world; indeed,
it's the only thing that ever has.

—Margaret Mead

We asked artist Alison Rash to create this art for us because she is a mom,
a cancer warrior, a former classroom teacher, an acclaimed artist, and
a person who shows us all that each of us can be a part of change through
our commitment, our work, our hope, and our love.

1
Becoming

OUR FRIENDS AND OUR ENEMIES SHAPE US.

Moments of conflict and collaboration form us, some hardening and toughening, and some softening and gentling. We are shaped by events that sometimes spin around us, that seem beyond our control, even beyond our influence, by people powerful and distant, sometimes beyond the reach of our voices, who seem so indifferent to what we might say that speaking appears futile. All these encounters with the world transform us, sometimes dramatically and suddenly, but more often gradually, almost imperceptibly into who and what we become.

Our friends and our enemies shape us, *but* they don't mold us inexorably, unless we allow them to. Events great and small affect us, influence us, but we aren't metal to be hammered into whatever shape the smith chooses for us, to become stronger or weaker, sharper or duller, only by virtue of the skill and purpose with which he wields his hammer. Nor are we clay tossed on the potter's wheel to be given whatever shape the potter's hands—events, circumstances, chance, fate, or whatever the force may be—choose to give it. We have, or we might have if we choose to, influence over that shape.

As the beginning of the decade has shown us, our lives are shaped by others and by events. The murder[2] of one man awakened international outrage about his killing and so many like it. The troubled and troubling political situation in the country aroused fears not only in the United States, but also around the world. And the COVID-19 pandemic changed schooling, and perhaps all of society, in ways that we are still coping with and just beginning to understand. These forces will shape us, but unless we are passive and despairing, abandoning all responsibility, we need not be metal under the smith's hammer or clay in the potter's hands—we will have much to say about the shape we will take and possibly the shape our country takes.

We have all been shaped by recent events. But in our response to them—what we think, say, write, and do—we participate in determining the outcome. How we make sense of the events— and that means making sense of what we read about them—will determine the shape of things to come.

We Are Forged, But We Do the Forging

It has been said that books change us, and certainly they might, but perhaps it would be better if we thought not that books change us, but that *books give us the opportunity to change ourselves.* We, the readers, should remain responsible for who and what we become. If we let books change us, forge us into what their authors want us to become, we will have turned responsibility for our own lives over to others. We will think what someone else wants us to think, believe what someone else tells us to believe, value what someone else tells us to value, and we will have abandoned ourselves. We will then truly be metal under the smith's hammer or clay in the potter's hands.

---

[2] We acknowledge that no jury has yet reached that verdict in the case of George Floyd. The verdict may ultimately be for something less than murder, but in our minds the act will remain a murder.

On the other hand, if we don't submit to texts, but rather take them in, reflect on what they have offered us, test their visions and understandings against our own, assess what we have brought to them and what they have offered us, and do that responsibly, willing to accept what is good and reject what is bad, and willing to reshape our own thinking, then reading will not simply forge us, but will enable us to forge ourselves, to shape ourselves into the best people we can become.

> **The books, the texts, do not and should not shape us. Rather, we should take the responsibility for shaping ourselves, *through the process of reading those texts*, through the act of taking in the words on the page, responding to them, considering our responses and our judgments, and shaping our thoughts responsibly.**

And so, it is significant that the title of this book is *Forged by Reading*. It is not *Forged by Books*. The books, the texts, do not and should not shape us. Rather, we should take the responsibility for shaping ourselves, *through the process of reading those texts*, through the act of taking in the words on the page, responding to them, considering our responses and our judgments, and shaping our thoughts responsibly. It is the act of reading, not the text alone, that shapes.

From a Moment to a Movement

All these moments in our lives—small and monumental, public and private—are just that: moments. The reading of a poem, even the reading of a longer work, an article, or a book, is just a moment, a small sliver of our lives. Most such moments pass and are forgotten. We watch an amusing but inconsequential television show and the next day can't even remember what it was. But some of our moments should have lasting effect.

Rather than pass and fade into oblivion, there should be something that we take with us, some change—perhaps slight but maybe significant—in our thinking or in our attitudes and values. Some of our reading shouldn't simply pass the time and then fade away, but it should allow us to change ourselves, rethink and reshape who we are and what we will do. Such reading might clarify, change, or strengthen our commitments. And those commitments, especially if they have to do with serious social issues, will align us with movements. If we want these moments to become movements, we must hold on to them, reflect on them, and then create the agendas to help them—help us—move forward.

School has often focused on moments. History is too often taught as a series of moments. We study the Civil War and then move on to World War I without giving much thought to what that moment from 1861 to 1865 might reveal about the fragility of our nation, its democracy, its values, and the commitments it will require if it is to be preserved. The Civil War remains little more than a moment, and then passes with little effect on the thinking or commitments of many of the students. The students at Marjory Stoneman Douglas High School knew that the Parkland shooting could remain nothing more than a passing moment, but it strengthened their commitment, and they tried hard to transform that painful moment into a movement.

After the murder of George Floyd, we watched thousands of teachers reach for books on antiracism, but reading a book and then reshelving it will not eliminate racism. Reading the books and then considering what they imply, reflecting on our own attitudes and beliefs, and committing ourselves to act and live in accordance with the principles and values we have responsibly decided are our own, might, on the other hand, result in more who are antiracist. When people reject bigotry, they become part of the movement, and if enough do so, the movement might lead to a better society.

There is no question that these books are potentially powerful— *Separated: Inside an American Tragedy* (Jacob Soboroff); *Stamped from the Beginning* (Ibram X. Kendi); *The Heartbeat of Wounded Knee* (David Treuer);

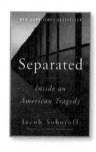

Cultivating Genius (Gholdy Muhammad); *The Crisis of Connection:*
Roots, Consequences, and Solutions (edited by Niobe Way, Alisha Ali,

Carol Gilligan, and Pedro Noguera); *Red Summer:*
The Summer of 1919 and the Awakening of Black
America (Cameron McWhirter); and *How to Be*
an Antiracist (Ibram X. Kendi). But their power
will not be realized by those who read them, say
"That was important," or even "That made me
think," and place them back on the shelf. Their
potential will not be realized if they are treated as
passing moments. Instead, readers need to say to
themselves, "These books give me the opportunity
to think again and anew about a significant issue,
they may help me see the world and myself more
clearly, and I may change what I value and what I will do as a result."
It's possible for adults who are not too set in their ways to do that.
We saw it happening as we attended webinars, Zoom meetings, and
Facebook Live events to discuss what these books meant to all of us.

That reading and that talking helped many people begin to
reshape their thinking and thus their lives. Those small shaping
moments for individuals, if enough individuals are involved, may
become movements. If we teach kids to read and think responsibly,
to be willing to defend the defensible and change what needs to be
changed, the students who leave our schools may be able to move
us toward a more inclusive society. In July 2020, Marc Morial, former
mayor of New Orleans and now president of the National Urban
League, watched his 18-year-old son organize a peaceful protest
supporting the ideals of the Black Lives Matter movement. His
son took the moment of George Floyd's killing and made it the
key element of a movement. Ruby Bridges, who sat alone in a New
Orleans school for her first-grade year because no white parents
would allow their child to be in a classroom with a Black child, turned
that yearlong moment into a lifetime of activism. She became part
of a movement toward justice, equity, and equality, devoting much

of her life to it, and she continues even today to be part of the Black Lives Matter movement.

If all those texts we read this summer, if all those webinars we attended, if all the television specials we watched, and conversations we had are to be more than passing moments in our lives (as important as those moments might have been), if we are to be forged by our reading, then we must individually and collectively decide what we value, what deserves our commitment, and what movement we support, in our lives, in our schools, and in our communities.

At this moment as we write, while the pandemic sweeps across the nation, while the evils of racism and bigotry are so glaringly obvious, while corruption and dishonesty in government are the norm, while the very environment is decaying around us, some of those values and commitments are predictable for many. Reading and reflecting on those issues will raise questions that might well be considered by faculty and students.

On the issue of racism, for instance, you might discuss in faculty meetings:

- What do teachers, administrators, and staff in our school think it means to be racist?

- What is our understanding—individually and collectively—of terms such as *prejudice, discrimination, racism, antiracism, micro-aggressions, segregation,* and *inherent biases*?

- What is the difference in being not racist and antiracist?

- Is our school ready to say "Black lives matter"? Do some still argue that "Well, all lives matter"?

- What have we done as a faculty to critically examine our curricula for white privilege? Is change met with the resistance that "We have always read this book"? or "We can't talk about such issues at school"?

- What examples of systemic biases do we see in our school policies?

- Do the curriculum we follow and the materials we use uplift the lives of BIPOC?

- Are teachers moving beyond understanding white privilege to understanding how white privilege affects classroom dynamics?

- Do some teachers in our school think "color blindness" is the goal? How do we address that in nonconfrontational ways?

- What do we tell ourselves about students or groups of students that might affect how we interact with them, evaluate their work, and respond to behavioral issues?

But to have read the books and then not considered what changes might need to be made is to have received but not responded; to have seen the reading as a powerful moment but then not have been committed to movement.

At the beginning of this chapter we said, "Our friends and our enemies shape us," *but* they don't mold us inexorably, unless we allow them to. We are not merely the potter's clay. We are also the potter. And as we shape ourselves into the people we want to be in this world, and as our students do the same, our books are tools that help us. Books, and the conversations we have with one another about them, provide us the moments that we might transform into commitments. If we and our students approach those moments with an open-minded willingness to embrace the new, a humility that lets us consider changing thoughts perhaps long-held, and if we remind ourselves daily that each encounter with a text offers us the possibility of seeing ourselves and the world more clearly, we may realize the transformative potential of literacy.

We don't know how any child's life will play out in the world, but we may hope that all of our students will realize that they are both the clay and the potter, both the metal and the smith, and, although they are shaped by the world that swirls around them, they, too, have a hand in shaping themselves.

2

A Meeting of Minds

FOUR THINKERS—A SCHOLAR NOTED FOR HER WORK in multicultural literature, an economist, a neuroscientist, and a historian—helped forge our thinking. Though working in diverse fields, in studying the work of each, we found common touchpoints, places where their work converged. This interconnection in their thinking was based on the role of language in shaping our society and thus the world in which we live.

Rudine Sims Bishop

We hope that at some point in your reading life, you've chosen to read one of the many scholarly works by Rudine Sims Bishop, Professor Emerita of Education at Ohio State University and the 2017 recipient of the Coretta Scott King-Virginia Hamilton Award for Lifetime Achievement. Her seminal essay "Mirrors, Windows,

and Sliding Glass Doors" (1990) should be required reading
for all teachers.

One of the many
books by the
award-winning
scholar Dr. Rudine
Sims Bishop

Rudine Sims Bishop has always written and spoken about
the role literature can play both in teaching us about ourselves
and in teaching us about others. Books, she argued, could serve
as mirrors, in which we see ourselves reflected, allowing us to
reconsider who we are, what we think and feel, what we value.
At the same time, books can be windows, "offering views of worlds
that might be real or imagined." Those glimpses of other worlds
might be merely entertaining and enjoyable—the escape into
imagination that fantasy offers, for example—or they might offer
powerful lessons about lives very different from our own and
include experiences that we may never have. If we learn well, and
are imaginative enough, and are willing to exert the intellectual and
moral effort required, they may even, she suggests, be sliding glass
doors, through which we may step, at least imaginatively, into the
worlds of others and the lives of those whose experiences differ
from our own.

The grave injustice Bishop's work addressed is that some readers
often see images of themselves in the mirrors; others seldom do.
Some look through the windows and see people just like themselves;
others see no one like themselves, or worse, distorted images and
fraudulent representations. Some step through the sliding glass door
into a familiar world; others step into a world from which they have
felt excluded and in which they feel uncomfortable. For years, we
have thought that the humanities would humanize us, that through
literature and art we would come to appreciate the diversity of human
experience and learn to accept and respect our differences and
similarities. Reading should help us become better—kinder, more
thoughtful, more willing to try to understand one another.

It has rarely worked that way. It hasn't, in part, because too many
of our students didn't find themselves or anyone like them in the
books they read. They looked in the mirror and saw nothing. Or,
worse, they saw a representation of themselves that was contrived,
narrowed, stereotyped. The reflection they found there was, as Bishop

wrote in her essay, "distorted, negative, or laughable." Accepting it would lead to a diminished view of themselves; rejecting it, to anger or despair. And those who looked into books and saw only their own limited experience, their own narrow world, were deprived of the opportunity to learn about others and deluded into thinking that they and others like them were all that mattered.

The humanities have not always yielded more humane people, in part, because we haven't always taught our students to read with the possibility of change in mind. We've taught them to remember details and analyze literary techniques and the other niceties, but we haven't always taught them to reflect on the implications of text for their own lives. Books won't change people. But people might change themselves if they learn to read responsively and responsibly. Our idealism need not be abandoned, as Bishop explains at the conclusion of her essay:

> Those of us who are children's literature enthusiasts tend to be somewhat idealistic, believing that some book, some story, some poem can speak to each individual child, and that if we have the time and resources, we can find that book and help to change that child's life, if only for a brief time, and only for a tiny bit. On the other hand, we are realistic enough to know that literature, no matter how powerful, has its limits. It won't take the homeless off our streets; it won't feed the starving of the world; it won't stop people from attacking each other because of our racial differences; it won't stamp out the scourge of drugs. It could, however, help us to understand each other better by helping to change our attitudes towards difference. When there are enough books available that can act as both mirrors and windows for all our children, they will see that we can celebrate both our differences and our similarities, because together they are what make us all human.

We have a long way to go before "there are enough books available that act as both mirrors and windows for all of our children." We must hear Rudine Sims Bishop's words as an urgent call to action, one finally to be answered.

Daniel Kahneman

Born in 1934 in Tel Aviv, Daniel Kahneman won the 2002 Nobel Prize in Economic Sciences. In 2013, President Barack Obama awarded him the Presidential Medal of Freedom. In 2018, he was named a Gold Medal Honoree by the National Institute of Social Sciences. One of his books, *Thinking, Fast and Slow,* received the National Academy of Sciences Communication Award for the best book published in 2011. While we both enjoy reading widely and outside our professional field, when we stumbled across this book in an airport bookstore, we were not prepared for how much it would affect our thinking about *learning.* His contributions to the field of economics are most easily summed up as research into how we make decisions. Perhaps this interest was sparked when he was a young boy:

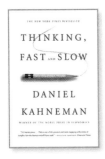

> It must have been late 1941 or early 1942. Jews were required to wear the Star of David and to obey a 6 p.m. curfew. I had gone to play with a Christian friend and had stayed too late. I turned my brown sweater inside out to walk the few blocks home. As I was walking down an empty street, I saw a German soldier approaching. He was wearing the black uniform that I had been told to fear more than others—the one worn by specially recruited SS soldiers. As I came closer to him, trying to walk fast, I noticed that he was looking at me intently. Then he beckoned me over, picked me up, and hugged me. I was terrified that he would notice the star inside my sweater. He was speaking to me with great emotion, in German. When he put me down, he opened his wallet, showed me a picture of a boy, and gave me some money. I went home more certain than ever that my mother was right: people were endlessly complicated and interesting (Kahneman, 2003, p. 417).

This interest in people being "endlessly complicated" morphed into a fascination and a lifetime of work regarding how we make decisions. That work was explained for us nonscientists in his award-winning and landmark book, *Thinking, Fast and Slow.* In this book,

Kahneman offers us a simple way of understanding how the brain makes decisions.

Put even more simply here in our book, he explains that we spend much of the day doing thinking that requires very little energy or discipline. We see a stop sign and stop. We see clothes that need to be washed and gather them for the washing machine. We see four quarters and know that means we have a dollar. Some of us have measured a teaspoon of vanilla so often, we don't need the measuring spoon. A lot of our thinking is fast.

But sometimes we must slow down. The thinking requires more effort. We must concentrate. To illustrate, think about what this sentence means: *The old man the boat.* Some of you might need to read it again: *The old man the boat.* At this point, a group of you have decided to keep reading, hoping we will explain it. But some of you don't want us to. You like riddles. You want to figure it out.

And that's a critical point for this book. Slow thinking, thinking that requires searching through all those file cabinets in our minds, is something we do *if* we like what we're thinking about. If you don't care about *Beowulf,* then sticking with a translation—even a good one—might not be worth the cognitive effort and you may decide it is "boring." If you've decided you don't "believe" in climate change, then you don't want to put forth the mental effort to think critically about your how your own beliefs align with scientific facts. If you don't really care how to calculate the diameter of a circle, then the thinking you must do to learn that is too slow for you to find it enjoyable. We like fast thinking unless, and this is the critical part, we are enjoying the slow thinking or are committed to questioning our understandings.

Much of the slow thinking we need to be doing now means reexamining our own long-held values and beliefs. We must be comfortable with uncertainty, with doubt, with the tension of not knowing, of not immediately "getting it." Why is this important to

> **"We must be willing to hold incompatible ideas in mind—incompatible because they do not match with what we are now learning. We must be able to unlearn so we can relearn."**

us? Because this is a time in our nation's history when we must all grapple with uncertainties and doubts. Many of us must be willing to doubt information, values, and systems we grew up with. We must be willing to hold incompatible ideas in mind—incompatible because they do not match with what we are now learning. We must be able to unlearn so we can relearn.

We must embrace an educational system that demands thoughtful reasoning about complex ideas. Covering material quickly so students will be ready for the test must no longer be the mandate of a district. Teachers must be allowed to let students sit with ideas, consider them, learn to live in the tension of ambiguity because binary thinking results in only binary answers. And binary answers will keep us a divided country, one that serves some but never serves all.[3]

Maryanne Wolf

Maryanne Wolf, author of *Tales of Literacy for the 21st Century* (2016), speaks of "the written word as the basis for generating new, never-before-encountered or shared thought" (p. 135).

We couldn't shake that sentence, and all the ideas it created for us, from our minds. If Wolf is right, then there are implications for us as teachers of reading. If she is right, then we should be thinking not just of leading our students to extract well from texts, not simply of teaching them to grasp what the writer has said, not just to comprehend, paraphrase, and remember what lies on the page, but to create the "new, never-before-encountered thought." The 10-question quiz we might have prepared for Friday seems hopelessly inadequate if our goal is the "never-before-encountered." Those 10 questions were only about what had already been encountered in the preceding four days.

---

[3] So, back to *The old man the boat.* If you are still wondering, by any chance, what that means, think of *old* as a noun, not an adjective, and *man* as the verb meaning "handle." You have to pause slightly between *old* and *man*— "The old [slight pause] man the boat"—for the sentence to have meaning.

The vision of reading that Wolf suggests emphasizes creation over extraction. The quiz emphasized extraction over creation. That quiz may have told us if the students extracted accurately and recalled material for three or four days, but it probably told us little about the students' abilities to go beyond extracting. We might see that they could remember the names of one or two of the characters, but the quiz doesn't reveal if students could see similarities and differences between the character and their friends, or themselves. It didn't show if they had changed their minds in any way about themselves, about human relationships, about the ways in which they had interacted with others around them. It didn't show that there was anything new in their minds or hearts after the reading.

The quiz showed only that they had done their homework and more or less paid attention in class, not that they had meaningful, personal thoughts. And reading should involve that thinking, that slower thinking Kahneman suggests. The 10-item quiz showed that they had received, but not that they had generated. It is too easy to slip into thinking if they have *received* well, we have taught well. But in Wolf's vision of reading, we had barely taught at all. We had not adequately encouraged them to move beyond the text, to lift the words off the page, to escape the confines of the four corners of the page, to bring the text and their own minds together so that they might see what would spring from that meeting. The power of reading lies in that meeting.

In 1938, Louise Rosenblatt explained in *Literature as Exploration* that meaning emerges as the reader interacts—or to use her word— transacts with the text. Without the reader's thoughts, memories, associations, and connections that come to mind while reading, the words remain merely inkspots on the page.

Wolf echoes Rosenblatt's thinking as she explains that these thoughts we have as we transact with the text might transform into new thoughts, never-before-considered thoughts. Thus, through reading, we become more than we had ever considered being.

Yuval Noah Harari

We were also influenced by the work of Yuval Noah Harari, an historian from the University of Oxford who, as of this writing, is teaching history at the University of Jerusalem. One of his books, *Sapiens: A Brief History of Humankind* (2015), has been read worldwide. In it, Harari contends that the appearance of civilization, large groups of people living and working in concert, depended primarily upon one development: "The secret was probably the appearance of fiction" (p. 27).

He offers a much more complex argument than that simple, eight-word statement suggests. By *fiction* he means *imaginative conceptions,* not the novel or the short story. One example of an imaginative conception is *money*. Money doesn't exist in the natural world. Humans imagined it into existence. Gradually, over thousands of years, the concept evolved and took root, and coins, then pieces of paper, then pixels on computer screens became tremendously significant to all of us. We can't eat it, like apples; it doesn't eat us, as do tigers; but it is a crucial part of the world we live in.

And yet it is still a *fiction,* a concept human imagination brought into the world. So, too, are the concepts of *human rights, freedom, justice, virtue, evil, gender roles, race, values, laws, traditions,* and others. *Justice* exists in the world. But not because it is part of nature. Rather, humans conceived of it, spoke about it, wrote and read about it, and thus created it. *Justice* is a human invention, an imagined part of reality. And *justice,* unlike gravity and the speed of light, continues to change as the human mind changes it.

Harari's work had profound influence upon us. Conceptions of race, of marriage, of power, are fictions. In this country, these fictions were written by white people. Reenvisioning the world— or, closer to home, our school curricula—means recognizing that some of our fictions are horror stories and must be examined, excised, and rewritten.

All Together Now

Bishop shows us the power of reading. Her vision of books as mirrors, windows, and sliding glass doors should be etched into the entryway of every school. Kahneman shows us that thinking is hard and helps us understand why we default too quickly to emotional answers rather than logic-based answers. Wolf explains how reading enables us to produce new ideas and how writing allows us to share them. Harari argues that it is through this creative thinking that we can reinvent our cultures, our laws, our traditions. We can right our wrongs.

> **If we are to reshape the world, those aspects of the world that are created in imagination and language, then we need to see reading and writing as opportunities to change.**

If Bishop's understanding of the power literacy offers is correct; if Kahneman's conclusion that we must discipline ourselves to slow down and deal with complexity is valid; if Wolf is correct, and the written word can be the basis of new, never-before-encountered thought; and, if Harari is right, that much of our reality is in our imagined conceptions, then we have much to do. The written word, well read, could yield new ideas which might be crafted into new conceptions that might change the reality in which we live. The change may be gradual and slight, may take many generations, but it may be possible for us to reshape the world.

We have already seen it happening. Dissatisfied with the conceptions of human rights that we have inherited, we protested the murder of one man who represented many more. Those protests rejected one vision of human rights and responsibilities and proposed another, more humane and inclusive. It is language that enables us to address those issues and—perhaps—to modify the world, the conceptual world, in which we all live. If we read both events and texts well, if we think well, if we speak and write well, our conceptions of human rights, racist actions, and all horrors of inequalities may evolve into something far better than what we have at the moment.

If we are to reshape the world, those aspects of the world that are created in imagination and language, then we need to see reading and writing as opportunities to change.

3

Sailing Into Tomorrow

TO EXTEND THE METAPHOR OF THE TITLE OF
the book, people who play with fire may get burned.

We can imagine that some will be nervous with the idea that kids
might generate new, as-yet-unimagined, never-before-encountered
ideas. We aren't sure what that means when we turn to teens. We're
comfortable with toddlers who invent new ways of eating their peas,
but what's a new, as-yet-unimagined idea for a teen?

And what if the new threatens the old, with which we've grown
comfortable? What if the as yet unimagined is unimaginably
frightening? Maybe you think, I don't want to encounter the never-
before-encountered; I'm having enough trouble with what I've
already encountered. Better, you may think, to stick with what you
have now. Our list of reasons for holding on to what we know is
endless: But we've always done it this way; I'm used to the way things
are; the devil we know is better than the devil we don't know; we'll
only make things worse; change takes time; fools rush in; don't leap

before you look; and so on. There are plenty of reasons available for those who don't want to change, who don't even want to consider alternatives, who won't even glance at a different possibility. The new might singe our fingers if we grasp at the unknown.

And the idea that in reading and writing we have the power to reshape not only ourselves, but also the conceptual world in which we live, the world of values, race, culture, guiding principles, social status, visions of good and evil or right and wrong—that, too, might worry some of us. If we rethink things, I may have to give up eating meat and I like my steaks; I may have to drive less and I love long, meandering road trips no matter how much gasoline I burn; I may have to leave my political party because I have reconsidered what it stands for. I may have to learn that I cannot say all lives matter until I believe Black lives matter. We may not want to face what close examination of our values, beliefs, associations, and principles might require each of us to face.

Sailing Over the Edge

These are legitimate worries. Accepting the new requires letting go of the old and familiar. Early sailors, thinking the world was flat, hugged the known coastline. They were fearful of dragons beyond the horizon. But some were willing to risk the dragons. These explorers embraced the new and unknown—at least the new and unknown geographically; tragically, they sailed with *their* vision of the social world, one in which they were conquerors rather explorers.

Sailing into tomorrow may require us to rethink assumptions and values so that we act differently in the future. There will be implications and consequences for considering the new and reconsidering what we have long thought. The only way to avoid the discomfort is to avoid the issues. If we can avoid talking about and reading about problematic matters, issues that might require us to rethink values and assumptions, then we won't feel the discomfort that such difficult thought might entail. If we banish from our

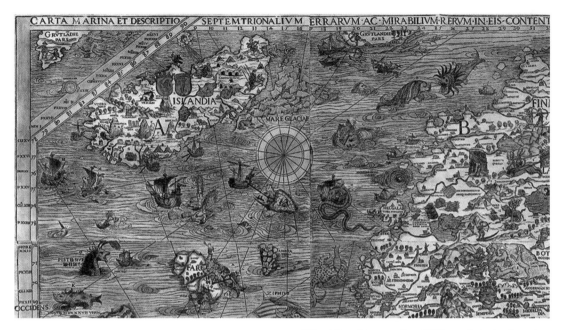

This old-world map, circa 1539, reminded sailors that
at the edge of the world, unknown monsters lurked.

minds, our libraries, and our classrooms any examination of politics, religion, race, environment, sex, justice, and the like, we might protect ourselves from the possible discomfort we might experience. All we have to do is trivialize the curriculum to the point that few will be bothered by anything.

Refusing to Rock the Boat

If we can make instruction completely insignificant, utterly irrelevant to anyone's emotional and intellectual life, then absolutely no one should rise up to protest the threat we pose to treasured beliefs, valued affiliations, or well-established habits of thought and action. We can teach kids how viruses are different from bacteria but avoid discussing why the health care system better serves the wealthy than the poor. We can teach what events led up to World War II and which countries fought on which sides and the horrors of the Nazi concentration camps but fail to mention our own concentration camps for American citizens of Japanese ancestry or consider why the 761ˢᵗ Tank Battalion or the 555ᵗʰ Parachute Battalion consisted solely of African American soldiers. We can give the facts of *Brown v. Board of Education* but never read what happened to the Little Rock Nine, never discuss how the integration of schools caused thousands of well-qualified Black teachers to lose their jobs because white parents refused to let their children be taught by a Black teacher.

We can teach the definitions of *preposition* and *conjunction*. That will raise few hackles. *Onomatopoeia* and *zeugma* are unlikely to drive marchers into the streets, even if we require students to learn both definition and spelling. Better yet, we can teach penmanship— that will threaten the values of neither the conservatives nor the progressives, neither Republicans nor Democrats, neither those drilling for oil nor the sailors on one of the Greenpeace ships.

Total irrelevancy, absolute insignificance, and unwavering stasis are effective strategies for avoiding the discomfort of thought and change. Allowing, even inviting, students to consider the new, never-before-encountered thought, might be seen as threatening the old. Even simply inviting them to know what we have too often failed to teach is threatening or confusing for many. We meet teachers who say, "The Tulsa Massacre, what's that?" or "The Trail of Tears, that was long ago," or "Who was Frederick Douglass?" "Do children really need to know about Ruby Bridges? About Harvey Milk? About the Stonewall riots?" "Juneteenth? Never heard of it." We are stunned when we say "Sonia Sotomayor" and too many say, "Who?" One pre-service teacher, barely out of high school, asked us "*Who* was Selma?" We do not blame her for her lack of knowledge. We blame a history we have too long failed to teach in this country. We blame a system that has too long hugged the safe shoreline of white privilege.

> **❝Total irrelevancy, absolute insignificance, and unwavering stasis are effective strategies for avoiding the discomfort of thought and change.❞**

Rethinking Our Teaching

Inviting students to rethink and possibly reshape values and assumptions might threaten ideas that some hold dear. But if what we teach has no implications and no consequences, we should be safe. If, as we teach reading, we choose bland books, steer our students away from topics that might raise the temperature of conversation, avoid anything controversial, anything that might reveal disagreement or difference or bias, we should be safe from everything but mind-numbing tedium. We can devote our time to teaching students to sequence, compare characters, or write a better summary.

> **"If we are to be forged by reading, then we must hand students books that stretch their thinking and ask them to let the book be more than a moment in their lives."**

As books for children and teens take up more and more realistic topics, we see more "well-meaning" parents or policymakers step forward with well-intended help for the school. They tell teachers and principals: "We don't need innocent fourth graders reading a book with a gay character. No reason to bring that up at their young age." "That picture story book about the Muslim girl, we just don't have any Muslims here. Do they really need to read about those people?" "That book, *The Hate U Give*, it just presents one side. And the language! I never! And it's not respectful toward the police. I see no reason for teens to need to spend their time reading this." Few parents have complained that their worldview is under attack when students are asked to distinguish between *simile* and *metaphor*.

Almost everything that matters in education, however, has implications. If we are to teach reading, conceived as the encounter with texts and perhaps other readers, in which ideas are found, formed, and examined, during which we may confirm or change our thinking and our attitudes, through which we may come to understand and perhaps influence the way the world works, those implications need to be addressed. If we are to be forged by reading, then we must hand students books that stretch their thinking and ask them to let the book be more than a moment in their lives.

Even the simplest and most basic of our educational goals, those that precede and underlie the goals of the disciplines, have implications, often political. Long before we get to the difficult issues in significant texts, we encourage students to adopt attitudes and act in ways that will enable them to learn, to collaborate, to simply live in the societies that human life requires. Schools socialize kids. Some people have seen teaching toward these broader goals as attacks upon individuals or groups.

Many of those goals, only peripherally related to the content-specific goals of the curriculum, are fundamental. They have to do with helping children shape themselves into people who can function in society and who will be capable of the thought that reading, and the study of any of the disciplines, will require. And yet, when teachers urge students toward responsible behavior and thought, they have occasionally been attacked. Such teaching is seen as a condemnation of political figures whose actions and thinking aren't as responsible as we would expect of most kindergarten kids.

The Values We Hold

But even the most basic and obvious lessons have political implications.

If we teach kids to value kindness, don't we implicitly condemn those who promote cruelty and indifference?

If we teach kids not to boast, don't we implicitly condemn those who devote inordinate time to self-congratulation and self-glorification?

If we teach kids not to bully, don't we implicitly condemn bullying and any who indulge in it?

If we teach kids to value information, don't we implicitly condemn those who ignore information and create misinformation?

If we teach kids to be reflective until they have enough information, don't we implicitly condemn those who are immediately certain?

If we teach kids to reject bigotry, don't we implicitly condemn bigots?

If we teach kids to respect the diversity of human experience, don't we implicitly condemn those who reject all who are different?

If we teach kids to judge individuals on their unique qualities, don't we implicitly condemn those who judge based on stereotypes?

If we teach kids to value truth and honesty, don't we implicitly condemn those who lie?

If we teach kids to value evidence, don't we implicitly condemn those who fail to provide evidence for assertions or seek evidence for assertions they accept?

If we teach kids to value reason and logic, don't we implicitly condemn those who favor irrationality?[4]

"When the issue at stake is sensitive, the flames rise higher. Race, sex, gender, politics, religion, justice, human rights, gun ownership, the environment, the right to protest . . . matters such as these turn up the heat and increase the risk that we will get burned."

When we value something, anything, we implicitly, but necessarily, reject its opposite. It seems to us that we should be able to sustain values, such as kindness over cruelty, reason over irrationality, and honesty over deceit, without fear of attack. But the attacks will come.

Similar points could be made about all the other simple human virtues that the schools often try to sustain. Without some attention to these matters, the schools could not continue. Schools could not function as democracy needs them to function if they value cruelty over kindness, bigotry over inclusivity, fraud over fact, groundless assertion over logical argument, irrationality over reason, ignorance over knowledge, misinformation and deceit over information and evidence. And yet, when an enshrined individual or belief falls short, the teacher whose commitment to the values of education may be vulnerable.

Few of those more general teachings are limited to the teaching of reading. They say nothing of the difficult and more inflammatory

---

[4] Bob first presented this list at the 2018 NCTE convention during one of our sessions. For his thinking, he received a long applause. I have always called this list Bob's Beatitudes. While we generally share credit for all that is written in our books, I must give credit for this list to Bob and thank him for making it a part of *Forged by Reading.* —KB

Students and young people lead the rally March for
Our Lives in Washington, D.C., March 24, 2018.

issues that significant literature addresses. When the issue at stake is
sensitive, the flames rise higher. Race, sex, gender, politics, religion,
justice, human rights, gun ownership, the environment, the right to
protest . . . matters such as these turn up the heat and increase the
risk that we will get burned. Even such a well-documented scientific
theory as evolution, the validity of which is unquestionable, may be
gasoline on the fire.

But to avoid such issues, when they naturally arise in the course of
our reading or in the news of the day, is to take refuge in irrelevance.
When students were killed at Marjory Stoneman Douglas High
School, for example, students around the country and the world took
notice. Some began to read and write about violence and guns, they
staged protests and made their disgust with the lack of action from
adults known. More recently, as students watched the government
response to the pandemic, it was impossible to avoid discussing
the role of science and information, the necessity of responsibility
and cooperation in dealing with threats to the entire society. In the
months following the murder of George Floyd, it was impossible to
avoid discussing race and the racial history of our country. These were

dramatic moments that we could not ignore, but the same potential for relevance lies in the books we teach. We would do well to admit them to the classroom, despite their sensitivity, despite their potential for awakening passions. And we will do better with changing the questions we ask of such texts from "What literary device did the author use to reveal conflict?" to "What has changed or challenged your thinking?" The right books with the wrong questions will not move us forward.

And these issues—race, politics, violence, gender roles, renaming of military bases, the removal of statues, the flying of the Confederate flag, the wearing of a mask—all these topics will awaken passions and disagreements. In the chaos of a normal day of school (though we have no idea what "normal" is anymore), we understand the inclination to say, "We will stick to standards we must cover and avoid the disagreements these topics will arouse." But we can't. We must embrace a standard that says we will all sit in tension, in confusion, in discomfort, and listen compassionately. We will search for evidence. We will read all the histories we must read. We will understand that disequilibrium will make us unsteady, but slowly we'll find our footing.

Indeed, the great potential of education, one that in too many places we have not yet realized, is to submit those difficult matters to reasoned discourse. Schools offer, or should offer, the opportunity to read and write about what matters, bringing reason and evidence to bear upon tough topics, personal and societal, perhaps generating new, unforeseen perspectives and thoughts, and possibly even influencing the shape of values and attitudes that become part of our reality.

Avoiding the difficult issues deprives students of the opportunity to bring the power of language to bear upon what matters most, to use what they read and write to reshape themselves responsibly, and to perhaps influence, however slightly, the shape of the world.

We approach difficult issues by reading, listening, and wondering with others. But we most always begin by reading. And much of that reading is fiction.

4

The Truth of Fiction

HARARI WRITES OF THE ORIGINS OF CIVILIZATION, but his observations are significant for teachers today. In *Sapiens: A Brief History of Humankind* (2015), as we mentioned in Chapter 2, he attributes the possibility of civilization, the existence of large city-states and nations such as those we now live in, not to the invention of the wheel or the taming of fire or the domestication of large animals but to the development of something much closer to our concerns as teachers.

"The secret," he writes, "was probably the appearance of fiction."

Fiction, Not Fire, Started It All

That's a startling assertion, but if Harari is right, then this just might be what saves us. If asked what enabled the beginning of civilization, we probably would have answered *fire*. And fire did play an important role. It allowed food to be cooked, which allowed for easier and faster digestion, which meant more time could be spent hunting or scavenging for more food to be cooked. But we were still in the middle of the food chain. For the longest time, we waited on the scraps the bigger, faster animals left behind, if we could get there before the smaller scavengers.

We could, thousands and thousands (and thousands) of years ago, point at the carcass of a deer left by wolves who had had their fill. But we couldn't sit around the fire and suggest that if wolves hunted in that area yesterday, then perhaps they might tomorrow and that might mean we should gather there and wait. That type of speculative thought was yet to come. That type of thought—the imaginative creation of what might be possible—evolved into what Harari calls *fiction*.

As we read his words, we were surprised. While we have taught reading all our adult lives, with a great deal of that reading in the realm of fiction, we still had never thought that fiction was the genesis of civilization. We have valued fiction and, of course, its close relatives, such as poetry and drama. We've defended its place in the curriculum, we've justified offering it to our students, and we've explained or attempted to explain the important role it plays in shaping the mind and heart of the individual. We have taught how to read fiction closely, not only enjoying the story it offers, but the lessons it teaches, the craft of the author, the beauty of the language. Most of us who are English/language arts teachers value fiction highly. But, again, few of us have thought that the very existence of civilization depends upon fiction.

Perhaps that overstates and slightly distorts Harari's speculative and tentative claim. He did, after all, qualify the assertion with *probably*, and the word *fiction*, as he uses it, refers to more than the novel—though for a moment it was fun to imagine that *Make Way for Ducklings* (or its ancient relative from Aesop) started it all.

Harari speaks of *fiction* as the myths and conceptions, the imagined creations and visions that shape our lives. But for most of us, the word *fiction* probably called to mind the books lying on the table next to our bed or perhaps that section of the bookstore.

Or, it could be that *fictions* call to mind those little ones we might utter from time to time: "No, dear, I don't see any gray in your hair." "Oh, my Zoom camera isn't on because it's broken." "So, we're watching HGTV, again. I love to watch a couple look at three houses to see which one they will buy. Gripping. Oh, you say after that we'll watch a couple look for their perfect beach house? Can't wait!" What it did not do for us, until we read *Sapiens*, was evoke images of humans gradually moving out of caves to start building New York City. If anything, that was nonfiction.

From Physics to Fictions

Once we understood that by *fiction* Harari meant *imagined conceptions*, we came to agree. *Fiction*, broadly conceived, might actually be the bedrock of civilization. We have little choice about obeying the physical laws of our planet. Gravity doesn't care whether we believe in it or not. It is only when we anthropomorphize gravity that we can say whether gravity cares about anything or not. Physical laws aren't based on the fictions, the speculations, we create. To put it another way, it did not matter how many times Galileo was out-yelled by the Church; the earth is not the center of the universe, as Ptolemy and Aristotle had posited. It's just *not*. Physics is physics.

> **"We live in a world of discourse. All of these powerful forces—values, customs, codes—are made and can be remade with words."**

But the world we inhabit is in some ways more complex and malleable than physics. The world we live in is structured by values, beliefs, principles, customs, myths, religions, laws, and ethical codes, all formed in language. Richard Mitchell (1979) says,

> *The world out there is made of its own stuff, but the world that we can understand and manipulate and predict is made of discourse . . .* (p. 13).

We live in a world of discourse. All of these powerful forces— values, customs, codes—are made and can be remade with words,

The Hammurabi Code is considered to be the first laws to appear in written form.

even though we may no longer speak of many of these concepts that have become such an integral part of our understanding that they seem to us, like gravity, part of objective reality. We live in the physical world, granted; but at the same time, we live in a conceptual world. Some of those concepts are important only in your family: Does the tooth fairy visit your house? Do you go to mosque or synagogue or temple or church or none of those? Is there a particular food that is perhaps served out of a particular dish during a particular celebration? Family practices are part of what makes a family a family. But if that tradition is changed for one reason or another, the rest of the world is not affected, not even others on your block—unless you are the one who always brings your Great Aunt Martha's famous baked beans. Then some might notice.

Some of the values and customs we follow are only consequential to a few of us. Which dish must be used for Great Aunt Martha's famous baked beans? Some customs often are enforced by peer pressure: women who smoke while pregnant receive condemning looks. And some customs keep things moving smoothly—in a mall, we tend to walk on the right side of the aisle; and at an ATM machine, we step away from the person at the screen.

Some of our fictions are agreed-upon laws created for us long ago. There were laws that denied women the right to vote. There were Jim Crow laws that told Black Americans which water fountains to use, where to sit on a bus, what schools to attend. There are laws that give authorities the right to separate children from families and to keep them apart from one another.

But those laws are fictions, conceptions that humans have created and agreed upon. Richard Mitchell says it this way:

> *An idea of reality is what we devise and perceive through our language; reality itself is probably something else again* (p. 27).

The customs and laws that are so important to us have all been devised in language. And they can be undone with language.

Valuing Our Conceptual World

This conceptual world, a fictional world created by our society and ourselves, is as important as the physical. And most of us probably spend more time and energy thinking about that conceptual world than we do thinking about the natural. When was the last time you suggested at dinner, "Hey, let's talk about gravity?" You're more likely to speculate about what might happen with someone's marriage, who's getting what promotion, or what gas might cost next week. Marriage is a social pattern that we, humans, have devised. Our evolving understanding of gender reflects newly embraced social constructs. Consider this: corporations aren't part of our physical world. They exist only through legal documents. Conceived in language, they can be dissolved in language. And to show the full scope of the fiction Harari suggests—ideas conceived in language—in 2014, the Supreme Court decided that a closely held corporation could hold religious beliefs (*Burwell v. Hobby Lobby*).

Some of the fictions—realities we agree upon and convey through language—are quite helpful. We will stop at stop signs. We will drive on the right side of the road (if in the U.S.). We will follow the "Detour Ahead" sign even as our map tells us to go straight.

We don't spend much time contemplating the finite quantity of helium, but more and more we wonder about fake news, about laws regarding mail-in ballots, laws regarding who controls a woman's body, laws defining what exactly is meant by "use of force." Through grappling with such difficult questions, we will finally reach agreement about realities, conceptual realities, that will guide behavior until more questions arise and perhaps lead to different answers.

But such conversing, debating, and even arguing will be valuable only if we ground our thinking in evidence and logic. What we read, whom we read, how widely we read, are critical as we turn to texts to help us forge a better reality of ourselves and the world around us.

The Fiction of Compliance

Such thinking, though, can feel dangerous in a classroom. Students will be noisy as they share their thoughts; parents might become upset. Some teachers will opt for a more orderly classroom, one in which information is delivered by the teacher to the students. We understand all that, especially on a Friday afternoon in high school before a pep rally. We're not sure that's the moment we want empowered students. Perhaps some peaceful compliance is a better idea. We assign something, and students comply. The principal walks by and peers into the classroom. Heads are bowed over a book or an assignment, and all look engaged. She nods. We smile. But, too often compliance is mistaken for engagement.

In school, compliance is often rewarded with comments that she is a "good student," or he is "always helpful." Students earn the "Citizen of the Week" citation for following the rules cheerfully and with little nudging. Before we continue, let us be clear: we want kids and adults to be respectful toward one another. We abhor bullying, especially when it comes from adults in leadership positions. We do, however, look carefully at who has won the "Citizen of the Week" certificate and too often see it going to the cute kid, the one quick to answer, fast to volunteer, who is neatly dressed, whose homework is uncrumpled and always on time. *That* kid.

The quieter student or the louder student, the one with a million questions, the one who consistently forgets something, the one who stares into space, the one whose clothes are a bit too baggy or a bit too worn, who doesn't have a pencil, can't remember how to log on to whatever device needs logging on to, didn't do the reading, snaps when a classmate says anything—well, we rarely see that student awarded "Citizen of the Week."

What if the really quiet kid just heard her parents arguing that morning? What if the disruptive kid is acting out because since the pandemic a parent's job hasn't returned? What if that rumpled shirt is the only one left? What if the brand-new pencils brought in so proudly that first day of school couldn't last through November, but the chance to get more is gone? What if I'm asking over and over why this is important because I want to do important things? If I bounce up and down, will you see me? Let me give that a try. If I hide behind unwashed, stringy hair, will you notice I've disappeared? Can you help me come back? What if I'm there and need you to notice but don't have the courage, the will, or the voice to speak such intimacies to you. What if that "don't-give-a-damn" shrug means "talking will lead to crying and then all things will fall apart"? What if defiance is the beginning of another John Lewis who understood the power of getting into "good trouble"? What if all those kids are being the best they can be, but their actions don't match our expectations? What if our expectations—our fictions, our perceptions, our beliefs—not our kids, are wrong? Are we willing to change?

The Labels We Offer

Students who don't so easily bend, who aren't as compliant as a teacher might want on a given day, are often given labels. The least harmful labels include *active, busy, high-energy, all-boy, strong-willed, inattentive, daydreamer,* or *quiet.* When the perceived lack of compliance continues, the descriptions become harsher: *doesn't mind, doesn't listen, won't follow directions, impulsive, thoughtless, unfocused, careless, won't participate in class,* and *distracted.*

And once those children simply don't behave the way we want them to behave, then the harshest labels arrive: "ADHD," "requires special attention," "troublemaker," "sarcastic," "rude," "disruptive." They are no longer disturbing others, but *are* disturbed; no longer quiet, but sullen and withdrawn; no longer unfocused, but unmotivated. That funny kindergartner who squirmed a lot has, by third grade, been pulled out and sent to the principal's office.

Many of those labels are fictions that come from our own perceptions of appropriate behavior. Labels can hurt, especially when provided by those who won't see beyond their own lives to the lives of others. The language we use reveals the truths we live. And when we discover those truths are nothing but fictions that need to be revised, we have the power to do so, if we will.

Just as we need to examine the conceptions through which we see our students, so must we invite the students to examine—and reshape—the conceptions through which they view themselves, their classmates, and their world. The process of reading and learning is essentially the continual reforming of the concepts that matter to us. Just as teachers need to think carefully about the labels, the concepts they employ to understand and describe their students, so do the students need to continually think about the concepts that filter their world for them. They tend, just as we might, to see the world in simply dichotomies: "us" and "them." "Believers" and "unbelievers." "Republicans" and "Democrats."

Reading gives us the opportunity to rethink those simplistic distinctions, and perhaps to learn that the differences between "us" and "them" are fewer than we think. Reading, if we don't think of it simply as extracting information, enables us to take control of the concepts by which we organize and comprehend our experiences. Reading far beyond our own lives and experiences will do what Harari explained and help us create and recreate the vision of our own lives.

5
Lily

LET'S TAKE A LOOK AT WHAT HAPPENS WHEN
our perceptions about reading, our fictions of what makes it "good"
reading, are used to assess a student—in this case, Lily.

We were visiting a school in a high-poverty area of a large city.
This K–5 school had been in serious academic "trouble" from the
state because for many (and we mean *many*) years, its students had
consistently scored at the bottom of all students throughout the
state. The school's students were about 90 percent Black and 10
percent Latinx. We were relieved to see that there was an all-Black
administration and that at least 50 percent of the teachers were Black,
with the rest being white. All students qualified for free and reduced
breakfast and lunch. The hallways gleamed with highly waxed floors
and were brightly decorated with student art and student writing.
There was pride in the school and that pride was reflected in young
faces. Most classrooms had many books organized neatly into bins of
different colors. We learned later the importance of those colors.

To avoid a state takeover, the school had started using a reading
program that provided ongoing coaching for teachers, lots of reading
materials for kids, and a very detailed set of standards that students

had to master to move from one reading level to the next. At the time we visited, the school was in its third year of using the program. Teacher transfers from that school had slowed and student scores had gone up. The principal and staff, and most certainly the company that published the materials used, were all excited at the results. We were there to see the program in action.

Meeting Our Reader

The coach from the publishing company who had been assigned to this school gave us a quick tour of the school and then directed us to a first-grade classroom. We entered and were introduced to the class as "authors who write books for teachers." Their hands shot up with questions for us: "Are you famous?" "Do your books have pictures?" "Are your books turned into movies?" (Several waving hands went down when the answer to that last question was "No.") "Have you met Big Bird?" (Hands went back up when Kylene was able to reply, "No, not Big Bird, but I have interviewed Oscar!") Our favorite question: "Do you want to see where I lost a tooth?" led to the inspection of many mouths when we foolishly answered, "Well, sure!" even as the teacher gave us *that* look and slowly shook her head no.

We navigated the maze of questions the best we could, and then the teacher stepped in (thank goodness). "Lily," she said. Lily sat up straighter. "I've chosen you to read to our special guests." While others sighed, Lily jumped up and listened as her teacher said, "You can choose any book from the orange basket."[5] "Orange?" Lily replied. "Really?" She rushed to that brightly colored basket and quickly found the book she wanted, *Aliens for Breakfast*. The coach, Lily, and the two of us went out into the hall and sat at a small, round

---

[5] Quite honestly, we don't remember what the real color was. We do know that colors were used to represent levels of books. Lily could have been looking through a turquoise, purple, black, or blue bin for all we can remember. We do remember that the books in the bin we have called "orange" looked harder than the books in most of the other colored bins or baskets. Maybe they were crates. They were objects that held books, and Kylene is a UT Longhorn, so she decided the books were in a burnt-orange something. —rep

table with chairs especially made for first-grade bodies. Small first-grade bodies. Lily couldn't wait to begin reading to us.

This youngster was excited to show the visitors—us—her reading skills. She hadn't read the book before, so this was a cold read. As she sat down, she told us, "I have been dying to read this book! My friend, she read it, and she said it is so funny."

Kylene: So you haven't read it before?

Lily: No. This is the first time I got to choose from
            the orange books.

Her bright smile as she all but bounced up and down suggested to us that she was comfortable with reading to us—two strangers—and excited to dive into the book. The coach pulled out her notebook and pen and was ready to take notes. We scooted our tiny chairs closer and leaned in, ready to listen.

Her reading, to our ears, was perfect. She was decoding fluently. Her phrasing was in meaningful chunks. No word-by-word hesitant reading for this young scholar. More importantly (to us), she was giggling as she was reading. It's a funny book, if you don't know it. The story begins as Richard, the main character, looks into the bowl of cereal from a box labeled "Alien Crisp" his mom has poured for him, and notices that things are moving in the bowl. His mom is a lawyer and is rushing to get dressed and get out the door. She just wants Richard to sit and eat his breakfast. As Lily read that part, she stopped, looked up and told us, "My mom is exactly like that. When she gets in a hurry, you better do what she says!" As she returned to reading, she interrupted herself again after reading this exchange in the book:

> Richard put down his spoon. "Mom, where did you find this stuff? It's alive!"
>
> "Richard, your imagination is getting out of hand," said his mother. "It's a free sample. I found it in the mailbox."
>
> "But it's moving!"

As Lily read that last line—remember, this is a cold reading—
she emphasized "moving!" And then she started giggling harder.
She looked at us and whispered conspiratorially, "It's aliens!
Remember, the cereal is called 'Alien Crisp'? He's got aliens in his
cereal." Now she wasn't suppressing her giggles, and we couldn't
help but laugh with her.

Lily continued reading:

> "I don't think it's cereal," muttered Richard as she
> hurried out of the kitchen.

Again, Lily laughed as she told us, "He knows something is wrong
because it is going to be an *alien*." She continued reading:

> "I don't think it's cereal," muttered Richard as she
> hurried out of the kitchen. He picked up the cereal box.
> 'Alien Crisp' it said on the front. 'Crunchy, Munchy
> Aliens in a Box! Packed on the Planet Ganoob and
> Rushed Straight to You!'"

Lily paused again, "Gross! It really is aliens. But it's funny, too!
Imagine you are sitting at breakfast—we eat Cheerios—and an alien
was swimming in your cereal bowl." We were laughing with her saying
it would be funny or scary—we weren't sure which! But then the
coach interrupted:

Coach: Lily, how long have you been an orange reader?

Lily: My teacher said I could read it. She said I could
             pick from orange. And my friend, she is reading it.
             So I picked it.

Coach: Would you read this sentence again? [pointing to
             the sentence with the word *Ganoob* in it.]

Lily: Okay. Packed on the Planet . . . [Now Lily paused
             and slowly sounded out the word *Ganoob* so that the
             o made its long sound:/Ga-nobe/.] Packed on the
             Planet /Ga-nobe/.

Coach: You might not be ready for this book. You are not correctly decoding this word, she said as she pointed to *Ganoob.*

Lily: Let me try again. [This time Lily gave the two *o*'s more of a short sound, /Ganob/.]

Coach: You haven't learned the /oo/ sounds and aren't ready for this book. It's above your level. But don't fret. You'll get there.

Lily: [Lily didn't give up.] It has two *o*'s. Like in *book.* [Then she tried to pronounce it using that sound.]

Coach: It's okay. You're just not ready. But thanks for giving this a try.

Lily looked at us and gave us a half-smile. "I'm sorry I messed up. I thought I could read it."

"You didn't mess up a thing," Bob leaned over to tell her. She barely nodded her head.

The Things We Left Unsaid

We sat there knowing that one aspect of reading—accurate decoding of new words—was being overemphasized. Lily, by our quick assessment, was doing everything else well and merely had not decoded one word the way the coach expected it to be decoded. An invented word, at that. But not wanting to question the coach in front of Lily, we stayed silent. We wanted to tell Lily that we thought the literacy coach was wrong and that she was doing a fine job, that she was a great reader. We wanted to tell this coach that we thought she was applying a standard much too rigidly. *Ganoob,* after all, is a made-up word from a made-up planet.

Lily was reading with understanding. She was reading with intonation that caught Richard's amazement when he realized some aliens were swimming in his breakfast bowl. She was laughing. She was connecting the text to her own life. "It was one damn word, and a nonsense word at that, so *really?*" we wanted to say. But before we could say anything, the coach sent Lily back to her classroom with a promise to have a conversation with the teacher.

As Lily returned to the classroom, the two of us stared at each other. We had failed that kid at that moment. We had watched this coach impose her standards of perfection on this child, but the standards seemed inadequate. It suggested to us that the coach thought that reading could be judged primarily by the accuracy of the child's pronunciation of individual words. We also wondered if this coach held the unspoken belief that perfection in sounding out would help raise the school's better but still-low scores on the state tests.

We saw Lily later in the day as she was bouncing down the hallway on her way to art class.

Kylene: We really liked your reading this morning.

Bob: That's one of my favorite books.

Lily: It was really funny. I liked it, too. [pause] But I don't know my double-*o* sounds so I can't read it. I think Ms. Arnold was mad at my teacher for letting me read from the orange books when I haven't learned all my sight words or double-*o* words. But I thought I *was* reading it real good. Oh, it's /Ga-nube/. I know that now.

Kylene: Your reading was great. Why don't you keep reading it during your free reading time?

Lily: It's only called that. It's not really free. You have to read from your level. Hey! Could you tell my teacher that you thought my reading was great? Our teacher said you were special guests because you know a lot about reading. Can you tell her to let me read that book?

Bob: I'll tell her I think you would enjoy reading it a lot. Maybe you could check it out from the library and read it at home.

Lily smiled through the exchange, moving between a bounce from foot to foot and a few jumps up and down. We wanted to say more, but her teacher called her to rejoin the group so she wouldn't be late to art.

Confusing Accuracy for Reading

Later that day, when we finally had some time alone with the literacy coach, we mentioned that we were confused as to why Lily had to stop reading *Aliens for Breakfast*. She explained that students need to know 100 percent of the words they will read in the books at the next level *before* they can read a book at that level.[6] She explained that the books had been carefully leveled to take into account all the phonics rules students were learning as they progressed from level to level; additionally, they needed to be able to recognize sight words that would need to be read with 100 percent accuracy at a particular level. We asked if pseudo-words from planets that don't exist were on any sight word list. We asked if she had paid any attention to how much Lily was enjoying the story and appeared to be understanding the wry humor. We asked if she had listened to her intonation, her phrasing, her emphasis upon certain words, all of which indicated Lily's ability to comprehend and enjoy what she was reading.

"I hold students to a high level of accountability. I've talked with this teacher who has, in the past, let children read above a level when they are not ready for that higher level. It's the teacher. These children haven't been held to high standards and that's why they

---

[6] It occurred to us later that we usually don't know 100 percent of the words we encounter in some of the books we read. Not that we know what level we're supposed to be on.

have failed. They get used to being able to just get by. Well, no more. Our program holds them accountable." We thought she was pausing. But no, she was done.

Our argument with that coach—who was provided by the company that created the program—continued all the way to the president of the company.

There, we discussed what conceptions of reading were at play in this incident. One conception seemed to reduce reading to the application of discrete skills; the other, which seemed to be ignored, saw reading as a complex interaction between an individual and the text, taking into account interests, responses, personal history, the unique stories of the reader, the values, language, and culture, and much more.

Perhaps the examination of just what reading is was bypassed because the relationship between the two parties involved was defined in advance. The school, the teacher, and the student were defective, to be fixed, and the company and coach were to do the fixing. In retrospect, it seemed to us that a great deal of available knowledge was overlooked. The teacher knew the student; the student knew herself. The coach knew the reading system, but perhaps had no time or opportunity to get to know the student. As a consequence, the student may have felt left out, on the periphery. Sarah Fine (2019) warns us, "Students will never learn deeply if you don't invite them to bring their full selves to the table." Lily had perhaps not felt invited, or least not invited at that moment.

One thing that was clear to us was that literacy, for this child in this circumstance, was not about acquiring any power or control. And it certainly was not Wolf's conception of "generating new, never-before-encountered or shared thought." Instead, she was submitting to the power of the authority figure, the coach. Lily had selected the book, was reading it enthusiastically and responsively, was connecting it to her own experiences, was engaging happily with the adults present at the moment. She was, in other words, doing much that reading entails. But all that was cut short because she mispronounced *Ganoob.* Lily began thinking "I don't know" when before, moments before, a part of her identity was "I know." The inclusion of one word, *don't*, can change an identity, a vision, and a voice.

Perhaps the problem was simply that there were different ideas about what constituted good reading. Possibly, the problem was hierarchical—the coach had more authority and power than did the teacher. Maybe the problem lay in a definition of literacy shaped and informed by practices that overly value accurate decoding. Whatever the problem was, Lily was not being taught that the ability to read and write more and more complex and powerful texts would enable *her* to do things in the world. She was not being taught that reading could help her become who she might be in the world and, in that becoming, help shape the world (Beers, 2002; Beers and Probst, 2017; Freire, 1968/1970; Golden, 2011; Harari, 2018; Muhammad, 2019; Probst, 2001; Rosenblatt, 1938; Wolfe, 2008).

Failing Lily

The coach saw so clearly the rules of the reading program that she failed to see the child in front of her. Her biases about decoding correctness, maybe hers or maybe the program's that she was hired to support and espouse, overlooked Lily's self-determination to "try it again." It overlooked her joy, her understanding of the text, her excitement at being a part of a reading community with her friend reading the same book, and perhaps a bit of pride in reading for the two authors.

This coach reduced reading to something that is to be judged for "correctness" or "mastery" as she followed the list of rules of the program, rules that prevented students from moving to a higher level until they have mastered all the phonics rules or sight words that will be used at the higher level. How long has the concept of "mastery" been used in education?

Acclaimed Mexican chef Enrique Olvera says, "I want Mexican food to keep moving" as he discusses his goal of seeking constant innovation (Lindeman, 2018). Innovation, not mastery. He's looking for the new. The never-before-conceived. He's not trying to master the making of a certain dish. In *The Economic Other: Inequality in the American Political Imagination* (2020) Wynton Marsalis says,

> In order for you to play jazz, you've got to listen to them [the other musicians]. The music forces you at all times to address what other people are thinking and for you to interact with them with empathy and to deal with the process of working things out. And that's how our music really could teach what the meaning of American democracy is (p. 202).

Listen. Interact with empathy. Work things out. Nothing about mastery. Nothing about extraction. It's all about interaction. Lily, that dear child, was interacting with the text. She was listening to what the characters were saying. Laughing. Wondering how it would feel to see an alien in your breakfast cereal. We think Marsalis would say she is on her way to being the adult we need her to be. We don't know what her jazz instrument will be—surgeon's scalpel, judge's gavel, teacher's lesson plan, writer's pen—but she must learn to listen. To interact with empathy. To work things out.

Yes, becoming a reader is, in part, about learning how sounds and letters work. But what if our first vision of literacy was not about mastery, but rather about becoming? About moving. About working things out. About listening. About giggling and excitement. About compassion. About transformation. What if our first vision of reading is that reading empowers children to become all they can be so they can forge a better life for themselves, their community, and their democracy?

> **66 What if our first vision of reading is that reading empowers children to become all they can be so they can forge a better life for themselves, their community, and their democracy? 99**

What if, when we relegate reading to a level, to accuracy, to mastery, we are sustaining a vision where one is the leader and the other the follower? One holds the power and the other does not.

The reality: literacy *is* power, it's all about power; and that day, in that hall, that coach held power over that student.[7]

The suppression of literacy shows up in many ways. Sometimes it hides behind the soft voice and genteel smile of a coach who says—kindly even—that a child "just isn't ready" for this book or that one. If we tell that to our young, excited readers often enough, then reading becomes a practice of word-calling, and any mistakes are internalized as "I'm not ready" or "I can't."

Literacy has always been power. Traditionally, the most powerful were most educated and the least powerful were least educated.

Sometimes, we have sat there and watched the deprivation happen. We've all taught Lily, and sometimes we have served her well, and sometimes we have not. Luckily, the art of teaching is never mastered. We can each grow each day.

---

[7] Lily's story has a happy ending. When we got back to the office that created this program, we had a meeting with the coach and the president of the company. The president of the company agreed with us and mentioned that this particular coach had a tendency to be too much of a rule-follower and had too often pushed students back a level when a teacher had decided to let students move up. The teacher received an email from the president who nicely copied us. Her note, in part, said that the coach had a wrong understanding of when a student should be allowed to move to more difficult books, and if the teacher thought she was ready for *Aliens for Breakfast* and if the student wanted to read that book, then that's what she should read next. The teacher wrote back, also copied us, and said she had already told Lily that. "I wasn't waiting for your permission. You provide a program. I provide an education."

6

The Courage to Act

LILY'S COACH WAS, WE DO HOPE, EXPECTING that reading would become for Lily a way for her to see herself, see herself in the world, and see beyond herself. We think that was her long-term goal. Our concern is that her short-term goals—such as learning the /oo/ sound—might eventually burn away that joy, that excitement, that realization that reading can help us change ourselves. Those short-term goals reflected a vision of reading as something to get right and be done with.

When Good Intentions Go Astray

The possibility of change hasn't always been foremost in the minds of people—members of the community, teachers, parents. We know that in too many places and with too many people, education has been confused with testing, reading has been dominated by leveling, and writing has been relegated to what you do after you have done something else—read a book, completed a science experiment, concluded a history unit. Independent reading is often a time during the school day and not a mindset; writing is controlled by state-testing expectations. Joyful reading and exploratory writing are, of course, the goals, but often the standards stand in the way.

We also see that more and more students are told to read like writers and write like readers. Those phrases are helpful when we want students to look at a passage and study the author's craft or to look at their own writing and ask themselves how a reader might interpret what they have written. Those are the times to read like a writer or write like a reader.

Let's not, however, overuse those phrases. Remember to let kids—and let yourself—read just to read. Read like a *reader*: a hungry, avid, gulp-in-the-words, can't-wait-to-see-where-I'll-go-next, wondering, laughing, crying, please-don't-end-dear-book reader. Likewise, encourage kids—and yourself—to write like a writer: amble along, let words gush, be surprised where they take you, stare into space, try on this word and then that one, write a sentence, delete two, write again, revise, draw, think, wonder, stop, talk, be frustrated, be a caught-up-in-what-you-did-not-know-was-in-you writer.

> **"Independent reading is often a time during the school day and not a mindset; writing is controlled by state-testing expectations. Joyful reading and exploratory writing are, of course, the goals, but often the standards stand in the way."**

Let's teach kids to be responsive, responsible, and compassionate readers, ones who are courageous enough to look at themselves through the actions of a character who looks or acts as they do or to look beyond themselves through the characters who represent what they are not. And let's teach kids to be curious writers, ones who write to discover, not merely to repeat; write to find clarity from a mess of ideas; write to follow their emerging thinking, not a rubric or formula. Readers read. Writers write. And their inclinations are better indicators of what students should read and write next than any leveling system or rubric ever will be.

We know that too many think children can't read *these* books in this basket labeled with this color or this letter until they have proven they know all the words in *those* books labeled with that color or that letter. We know that books put into any "leveled" basket have all too often resulted in children carrying the label just as the basket does. "You can read from the H basket" is too often heard by children as "You are an H."[8] And we know that for some adults who think decoding precedes meaning-making, when those children shift from the former to the latter, the focus is on the meaning that might be found right there in the text, within the four corners of the page.

Independence and Empowerment

Those who have proposed that meaning resides within the boundaries of a page have a more limited view of literacy than we propose. We agree that meaning begins with the words on the page—that's why they are there. But they mean nothing until they move beyond the page to the reader's mind and heart. Until those words touch the reader and the world, they remain "inkspots on paper" (Rosenblatt, 1938). The view that meaning resides within the four corners of the page encourages us to teach the kids only to take that meaning, to receive what the text has offered, to get it right. It suggests that the writer has the wisdom, and the reader should accept it. The reader's job is to extract meaning already made.

---

[8] We do think leveled books serve a purpose during some small-group guided reading instances. These groups should be fluid and change often based on each child's growth in any particular skill area. But no child, ever, should hear a teacher say something like, "He's an H" to another teacher or "You are an H reader" to a child.

Sometimes that extracting is simplified so much that it becomes mere decoding. To the notion that independent reading is word-calling with automaticity, fluency, and no errors, and that the goal is to find meaning as it exists only on the page, we say that such pedagogy is dangerous and it has hurt our students and society. Furthermore, as we have taught our nation's children to answer questions—as complex as they may be—we have, too often, failed to teach them to question answers. To question authors. To question texts. To question those who demand acquiescence. To question anyone—especially leaders—who offer edicts without evidence. To question those who would lead without facts, divide rather than unite, and choose unfounded belief over science. When we don't teach students to question and possibly to create new and unanticipated answers, we teach them simply to accept what the past has given them and not to reshape it so that the future might be better.

An empowered reader, an empowered person, is one who dares to raise those questions. An empowered person is one who has the courage to stand against those who oppose empowerment of any individual or group. An empowered person thinks and acts with boldness and humility, with facts and with compassion, with language that is clear and thinking that is logical. An empowered person acts with self-determination and lives a self-determined life.

Too often, though, classrooms, society, culture, policies, and on and on have suppressed the empowerment of too many. We have relegated certain students to certain scripted programs, programs where students' answers are expected but their questions are left unvoiced and unexplored. We have failed to offer the most rigorous classes for all students, set the same high standards for all students, and encourage the same independent thought for all students. We integrated schools while we segregated expectations. And that is a suppression of power. This suppression of power by withholding of the right to read and write is nothing new. Sadly, it's not new at all. To change this, we must all muster the courage to act.

PART II
Power

It is very nearly impossible to become
an educated person in a country
so distrustful of the independent mind.

—James Baldwin

We chose this art by London Ladd because this young man represents, for us,
the independent mind we want to see in all children. Ladd's work appears
in critically acclaimed books, including *March On! The Day My Brother Martin
Changed the World* and *Frederick's Journey: The Life of Frederick Douglass.*

7

Power and the Suppression of Power

WE HAVE SAID IT IN THIS BOOK AND SAID IT FOR years at national conferences (ILA 2017; NCTE, 2017; NCTE 2018; NCTE 2019): literacy is power. That literacy is more than simply *reading and writing*. It is also *power and privilege*. Frederick Douglass offered the world a firsthand account of this truth.

Frederick Douglass witnessed, in his own life, the significance of a literacy of which he was being deprived. Enslaved and powerless, he lived in a world that was written for him by those who had the ability to read and write, and he wanted, passionately, to be able to shape himself and his world as only the ability to read and write would enable. And he achieved his goal. An abolitionist, a writer, an orator, a diplomat, a newspaper owner, and a strong supporter of women's rights, he recalled, in one of his autobiographies, *Narrative of the Life of Frederick Douglass*, what his master had said to his [the master's] wife upon learning that she had been teaching Douglass to read.

He wrote that his master said that if the wife were to continue to teach him to read,

> . . . there would be no keeping him. It would forever unfit him to be a slave. He would at once become unmanageable, and of no value to his master. As to himself, it could do him no good, but a great deal of harm. It would make him discontented and unhappy." These words sank deep into my heart, stirred up sentiments within that lay slumbering, and called into existence an entirely new train of thought. It was a new and special revelation, explaining dark and mysterious things, with which my youthful understanding had struggled, but struggled in vain. I now understood what had been to me a most perplexing difficulty—to wit, the white man's power to enslave the black man. It was a grand achievement, and I prized it highly. From that moment, I understood the pathway from slavery to freedom. It was just what I wanted, and I got it at a time when I the least expected it. Whilst I was saddened by the thought of losing the aid of my kind mistress, I was gladdened by the invaluable instruction which, by the merest accident, I had gained from my master. Though conscious of the difficulty of learning without a teacher, I set out with high hope, and a fixed purpose, at whatever cost of trouble, to learn how to read. The very decided manner with which he spoke, and strove to impress his wife with the evil consequences of giving me instruction, served to convince me that he was deeply sensible of the truths he was uttering. It gave me the best assurance that I might rely with the utmost confidence on the results which, he said, would flow from teaching me to read. What he most dreaded, that I most desired. What he most loved, that I most hated. That which to him was a great evil, to be carefully shunned, was to me a great good, to be diligently sought; and the argument which he so warmly urged, against my learning to read, only served to inspire me with a desire and determination to learn. In learning to read, I owe almost as much to the bitter opposition of my master, as to the kindly aid of my mistress. I acknowledge the benefit of both . . . . (p. 33)

Literacy and Power

Literacy gives power to those who hold it. That should be obvious from its troubled and occasionally bloody story. The history of literacy is largely the history of the suppression of literacy.

In the Middle Ages, for instance, the priests in Europe didn't want the *common* people—any of us—to be able to read. If we could read, we might read the Bible ourselves. And we might not read it as they, the priests, would have us read it. We might interpret it in our own way, or ways. We might come to depend less on the sanctioned or self-appointed intermediaries and more on our own relationship with the text. And that would potentially upset the order they were comfortable with, reduce their control over us, empower us. To keep the commoners unempowered, they were kept illiterate.

When our states were still becoming the United States, a person was considered "literate" if he could sign his name. Actually, you didn't have to know how to sign your name. You could just make an *X*. So, who held the power? The person who wrote the contract about selling your land and told you what it said, or the person who could only listen to what was read and then make his mark? It was quite fine with some that the ability to read and write complex documents was in the hands of a limited number. That kept those few in power.

By the time we reached the end of the 1700s, while the framers of the Olive Branch Petition, the Articles of Confederation, the Declaration of Independence, and the Constitution were able to read and write complex documents, most were literate if they could write simple words and read or write simple letters to others. The ability to write well—meaning penmanship—was a lauded accomplishment. Why? If you were out working in the fields, shoeing horses, working the mill, driving the cattle, planting the gardens, then when was there time for learning the calligraphy of the most learned? There wasn't. Again, the powerful had the time, and the powerful were the literate.

We still see holdovers of that notion that good penmanship is important. Many of us remember our first pads of cursive writing paper in which we practiced upper- and lowercase letters until we could form them perfectly. (Those of you missing this part of your educational history, don't be dismayed. You knew what TikTok was when we still thought it was a new flavor of Tic Tac.) Some today still proclaim that unless we teach cursive writing, children will not be—well, we aren't sure what they won't be. But back to long ago, the reading of complex texts was for only a few, and writing them was for fewer still—those who held the power.[9]

Black Americans and Education

Our nation's racist history is easily seen in the differing ways various groups of people have been educated—or not. Pre- and post-Civil War laws and practices existed to keep Black people illiterate. To teach a slave to read was, in many places, a criminal offense. Though today we speak of compulsory education, much of our history was committed to compulsory illiteracy for Black people. It was well understood that an enslaved person who could read and write would be harder to control, harder to see as less than fully human.

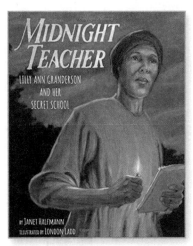

South Carolina, in 1740, passed a law forbidding everyone from allowing enslaved people to be taught to write. In Georgia, teaching slaves to read was outlawed in 1770. Frederick Douglass was just the sort of man southern legislators feared. In 1829, the Georgia prohibition against instruction in reading and writing was affirmed and extended to include "free persons of color." Other southern states had similar legislation. Virginia considered the literacy of slaves such a serious threat to the status quo that it instituted the possibility of the death penalty for slaves who violated the

Though it was illegal to teach enslaved people to read, there were those, such as Lilly Ann Granderson, who saw the power of reading. She risked her life as did her students—children and adults—in coming together to become readers and writers.

---

[9] In all of American history, Black people were the only ones denied by law the right to learn to read and write. Read more about this in *Black Ink*, edited by Stephanie Stokes Oliver.

proscription against learning to read and write, and serious penalties for whites who might dare to provide the instruction:

> *Following another high-profile armed uprising, the 1831 Nat Turner rebellion, Virginia strengthened its anti-literacy legislation so that the death penalty could be imposed for transgressions (Virginia 424; code 111, sec. 15). Virginia's slave codes became a model for anti-literacy legislation throughout the slaveholding South* (Rasmussen, 1970).

The conclusion of the Civil War and the Emancipation Proclamation did not put an end to the struggle for education Black people faced. The Thirteenth Amendment put an end to slavery and was ratified in 1865. Then, in 1868, the Fourteenth Amendment should have increased the legal rights of now-freed enslaved people, as it assured that no state shall deprive anyone of either "due process of law" or of the "equal protection of the law." By 1870, the Fifteenth Amendment prohibited states from denying freed slaves the right to vote. Undoubtedly important legal steps, these amendments to the Constitution did not change how Black people were treated, especially in the South. Southern states wrote laws, first known as Black codes and then known as Jim Crow laws, that explicitly outlined how Blacks were to be treated differently from whites. Black people, for instance, had to swear upon a different Bible from whites in court testimonies; a Black person could not marry a white person; Black people were prohibited from living in white neighborhoods.

In 1892, Homer Plessy, a Black man, refused to give up his seat on a train in New Orleans to a white man. Louisiana state law required he do that. He cited the Fourteenth Amendment and said that he was protected under the clause in that amendment that said all people, regardless of race, are due equal protection under the law. His case made it to the Supreme Court in 1896. The landmark decision in *Plessy v. Ferguson* resulted in Plessy's complaint being overturned. The majority decision, written by Justice Henry Billings Brown stated in part:

The object of the [Fourteenth] amendment was undoubtedly to enforce the equality of the two races before the law, but in the nature of things it could not have been intended to abolish distinctions based upon color, or to endorse social, as distinguished from political, equality. . . If one race be inferior to the other socially, the Constitution of the United States cannot put them upon the same plane.

While this was a blow and is inarguably one of the tragic decisions of the Supreme Court, what cannot be overlooked is the dissenting opinion written by Justice John Marshall Harlan. He wrote:

Our Constitution is color-blind, and neither knows nor tolerates classes among citizens.

This bold dissent would become the rallying cry for many. This is often the case with Supreme Court decisions, and leaves us to wonder why students do not read these decisions—especially more current ones—and most important, the dissenting opinions. The dissenting opinion is often offered by a Justice whose vision into the future is clearer than others. Perhaps it would do us all well to read decisions, both majority and dissenting opinions.

But *Plessy v. Ferguson* allowed the Jim Crow laws to continue and to keep schools segregated. While many fought to abolish Jim Crow laws, and particularly to integrate schools, it was the landmark case, *Brown v. Board of Education* that overturned *Plessy v. Ferguson*. On May 14, 1954, Chief Justice Earl Warren delivered the unanimous opinion of the Court, stating that

We conclude that in the field of public education the doctrine of "separate but equal" has no place. Separate educational facilities are inherently unequal. . . .

Declarations, laws, and mandates, though, rarely change systemic biases, racist beliefs, and long-held customs. And today, we still see in too many ways that the highest levels of education—the number of AP or IB classes, the experience of the teachers, the facilities of the school, the opportunities for support or advancement or counseling over expulsion—are found in schools in the highest income areas, and all too often those areas are filled with white people.

While much of the public knows some of this history (and what is presented here is only the smallest part of that story) of the laws denying Black people first the chance to become literate and then later the chance at the same education as their white counterparts, we too often fail to note that our nation's history of denying education to those who are not white extends to others.

First Nations People and Education

At the same time that white people struggled to keep Black people illiterate, they were grappling with how to treat the indigenous people of this land. The five First Nations peoples were forcibly removed from their land, herded across America, given treaties that were immediately broken by white people, and were discounted as the rightful heirs of this land. The easiest solution was assimilation, which ended up not easy at all. In the 1790s, Henry Knox, George Washington's Secretary of War, wrote to Washington of the Native Americans:

> *How different would be the sensation of a philosophic mind to reflect that instead of exterminating a part of the human race by our modes of population that we had persevered through all difficulties and at last had imparted our Knowledge of cultivating and the arts, to the Aboriginals of the Country by which the source of future life and happiness had been preserved and extended. But it has been conceived to be impracticable to civilize the Indians of North America—This opinion is probably more convenient than just* (Miller, p. 208).

By the 1860s, the U.S. had begun operating boarding schools for Native American children, taking them, often forcibly, from their parents to teach them "English" ways. These children were given new names, new haircuts, new clothes, taught a new religion, and were expected to learn to read and write English so they could work in a trade and read the Bible. First stripped of their land and then of their culture, First Nations children continued to fight for an education on their reservations that was equal to that of all others. To find an adequate education, however, too many were forced to leave their reservations and face the assimilation into the white culture insidious in our schools.

This biographical picture storybook tells the story of Zitkala-Sa who was taken from her village and forced into a boarding school. Overcoming that, she became an activist and composer.

Little changed over time. In 1969, a subcommittee of the U.S. Senate issued a report titled *Indian Education: A National Tragedy/A National Challenge.* The authors of this report mince no words as they wrote:

> *We have developed page after page of statistics. These cold figures mark a stain on our national conscience, a stain which has spread slowly for hundreds of years. They tell a story, to be sure. But they cannot tell the whole story. They cannot, for example, tell of the despair, the frustration, the hopelessness, the poignancy, of children who want to learn but are not taught; of adults who try to read but have no one to teach them; of families which want to stay together but are forced apart; or of 9-year-old children who want a neighborhood school but are sent thousands of miles away to remote and alien boarding schools.*
>
> *We have seen what these conditions do to Indian children and Indian families. The sights are not pleasant. We have concluded that our national policies for educating American Indians are a failure of major proportions* (p. xi).

In spite of the 60 recommendations made in this report, we have not done better.

Latino-Americans and Education

Simultaneously, early white America worked to keep Mexican children out of white public schools. When Mexico extended into what is the U.S., Mexican students attended Catholic schools or their own public schools. Their language, their culture, their beliefs were honored and respected. But as boundaries shifted, the question over education became problematic. White parents did not want the brown-skinned children in schools with their white children. And while the argument was, "Well, they don't speak English," the reality was whites, again, recognized that literacy is power. When some, mostly in Florida, put Mexican children into white classrooms, those children were only the lighter-skinned children of more affluent economic status, and it was expected that they would speak only English.

Again, we see that whether the white intruders were forcing one group to learn to read and write English or denying another group an education, the purpose was the same: to retain power. One of the best comprehensive histories we've read about the Latino struggle for education in the U.S. is titled "Demanding Their Rights: The Latino Struggle for Educational Access and Equity" by Victoria-María MacDonald (2013). In this, she traces the history of the people of Mexico working to secure an education for their children. It is worth quoting directly from MacDonald's history to show the full impact of the segregation forced upon brown-skinned children who merely wanted an education:

> Unlike the strict de jure segregated schooling for African Americans in the South based upon race, Mexican American children in Southwestern and Midwestern states such as Iowa and Kansas, were placed in "Mexican" classrooms or schools as a result of "color of the law" or "custom" beginning in the early 1900s. Anglo administrators defended this practice, saying that it was a result of English language deficiencies, although many "Mexican" students spoke only English.

Furthermore, Anglo parents objected to their children being schooled with what they called "dirty and diseased" Mexicans. Underlying the rationales provided for separating most Mexican American students from Anglo students was an ideology among the white elite that Mexican American children belonged to a different and lower-class system based upon the political economy of the Southwestern agricultural system.

Basic levels of education were viewed as a necessity for literacy and workforce skills. Higher levels such as secondary schooling and college, however, would permit Mexican American children access to a segment of society Anglos reserved for themselves. Nomenclature of schools is telling in this regard. Particularly in Texas, schools with mostly white children were called "American" while schools designated for children of Spanish or Mexican descent were called "Mexican" (pp. 309–310).

But Latinx parents rejected separate and equal. In 1925, four Mexican American high school students registered to attend a white high school in Kansas City, Kansas. Their names are rarely mentioned in any school: Jesus and Luz Alvarado (brothers) and Marcos De Leon and Victorina Perez. Saturnino Alvarado, the father of Jesus and Luz, wanted his two sons and their two friends to be able to attend a local high school.

The school board offered them a separate classroom with their own teacher. They declined that offer. They offered to send them— at the district's expense—to a school for Mexican American students in Kansas City, Missouri. They declined. After a year of negotiations that included the U.S. Department of State, the students were admitted. Other challenges were made and then, six years prior to *Brown v. Board of Education*, the Supreme Court heard the challenge from *Mendez, et al v. Westminster School District of Orange County, et al.* Mendez and five other families worked tirelessly for years to have the schools in Orange County, California, integrated. The Supreme Court agreed with their argument and this important case helped pave the way for *Brown v. Education.*

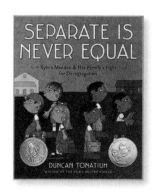

This briefest of histories does not even touch upon how Chinese, Japanese, Indian immigrants, or girls—of any race—were treated. What is important to note is how much is not taught to our students. We must ask ourselves if this is out of our own ignorance. Why were so few of us taught about George Mendez? Why did we not learn that Plessy, before Rosa Parks, refused to give up his seat? Why do some, but not enough, learn about Rosa Parks and the Little Rock Nine, but not, Jesus and Luz Alvarado and Marcos De Leon and Victorina Perez? Why do so many not know about Sequoyah? Some will claim ignorance saying, "Well, no one taught me." And, of course, that leads to the question, "Why not?" Are we looking closely enough at who authors our students' history books? Are we looking closely enough at what books, what people, which history we share? If literacy is power, then we must ask, of ourselves, what we each do to empower all.

In many schools and in many homes, historic and current systemic racism goes undiscussed. Now, with the urging of the Black Lives Matter movement, more white people than ever before are asking questions and building an antiracist agenda. White people must also examine our past and current actions toward First Nations people and all people of color.

This is difficult work, but we cannot begin to be better until we know better. To quote the person who said it best, Maya Angelou, "Do the best you can until you know better. Then when you know better, do better" (2009, personal notes of Kylene Beers while listening to Maya Angelou give a talk).

Literacy's Intrinsic Value

Those stories of the efforts by some to deprive others of power over their own lives and thoughts also serve as evidence of the importance of literacy. Those men who instituted the death penalty in Virginia's code clearly thought that literacy for slaves—and even for "free persons of color"—was a threat to the lawmakers' power and privilege. A century and a half later, those who shot a young Pakistani girl, Malala Yousafzai, for speaking out on girls' right to education, presumably thought that educating women threatened a social order they cherished, one in which men had almost all the power and women had almost none. All those men, evil as their actions were, valued literacy. They saw it as a source of their status, their higher position in society, their right to dominate, decide, rule, control.

Malala had some idea what education, what literacy, might do for her and her community. Those enslaved men and women, young and old, who were bought and sold on a master's whim, knew what literacy might do for them. In her study of the testimonies of enslaved Africans, Janet Duitsman Cornelius (2015) writes:

> *Reading and writing, above all, pointed the way to freedom—first of all in the mind and spirit, and often in the body. Slave testimony, therefore, illustrates how acquiring reading and writing skills was an act of resistance against the slave system and an assertion of identify by the literate slaves* (p. 43).

In the times leading up to the Civil War, southern whites wanted to retain literacy and its power for themselves alone. They fought hard, even to the extent of cutting off the fingers of those daring to learn to read, to keep literacy out of the hands of those who might employ it to assert their own humanity.

And those who were not granted literacy, as their right, fought as hard to attain it, in some cases risking—or suffering—torture and death. Both the oppressors and the oppressed demonstrated for us the value of literacy. Access to those 26 letters of the alphabet[10] and all that can be done with them, matters.

In the September 2020 issue of *Vanity Fair*, Ta-Nehisi Coates wrote, "To plunder a people of everything, you must plunder their humanity first." We must plunder their humanity first. White America has a long history of taking away humanity in so many ways from Black people, brown people, First Nations people, from anyone not white. But try as

---

[10] In our society and dominant language in the United States—the number of symbols and letters will be different in other languages.

many did to deny literacy, deny the power that comes from literacy, too often we failed. Thank God—whatever that power is to you—we failed. And those who succeeded made our nation stronger.

And yet, here we are today, astounded at the question we are hearing more and more often: "Why bother with reading?" As we sit stunned at that question, we know that we have videos, the computer, the television, and even, for the more ambitious, audible books. Reading is slow, inefficient, tedious, we are told. And the kids don't like it. For entertainment they prefer video games; for instructions they'd rather go to YouTube; for stories they have television shows or for short stories they have Snapchat; for longer stories they have television mini-series or they can go to the movies or stream them; for information about what's happening in the world they turn to their social media feed that tells them what an algorithm has figured out they want to know.

Granted, they come to school wanting to learn to read, but it doesn't take long for reading to lose its appeal. A look at Scholastic's *Kids and Family Reading Report* (2019) shows that between ages 8 and 9, reading interest shows a decline. This decline does not improve, leaving too many of our middle and high school students avoiding reading for recreation or learning.

Perhaps we have not managed to teach those students what both the oppressors and the oppressed understood—that literacy enables us to do something. It enables us to change ourselves, and it might enable us to change the world, if only slightly. From that speculation, that what-if, comes ideas that might bring about change. But if it is to give us that opportunity and that power, we have to ask ourselves what should happen next. It is that question that allows us to find out what it is that we might do. Malala had some idea what education, what literacy, might do for her and her community. Those enslaved men and women, young and old, knew what literacy might do for them. The adults who sit in adult literacy classes know. The children in faraway countries, walking miles to sit on the ground to learn to read, know.

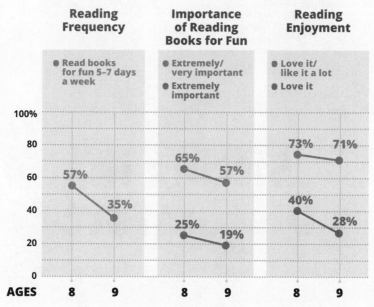

The Reading Decline from Ages 8 to 9

Base: Children ages 8–9

Reading empowers. And through that empowerment, with the right books, as Bishop explained, and with the right expectations, as Wolf explained, and with the willingness to be open to changing our minds, we create those never-before-imagined thoughts and help to forge an only imagined world. Scholes (1985) says:

> . . . reading and writing are important because we read and write our world as well as our texts, and are read and written by them in turn. Texts are places where power and weakness become visible and discussable, where learning and ignorance manifest themselves, where the structures that enable and constrain our thoughts and actions become palpable (p. xi).

More precisely, reading empowers our thinking if we have the energy and the will to do the necessary work.

8

Sitting in Discomfort

PERHAPS IF STUDENTS BETTER UNDERSTOOD THAT reading empowers them—even though the thought of empowered eighth graders on a Friday afternoon may scare us—they might be more willing to do that hard work. Critical, analytical, and deliberate thinking is only too hard when it is not meaningful. How many times have we heard, "Why do I have to learn this?" We interpret that question as a search for relevance.

Encouraging our students to participate in the shaping of the unknown future is the goal. Rather than teach them to receive what the past has given them, to absorb what history, family, community, and culture have imposed upon them, we should require students to take all of that raw material and reshape it responsibly for themselves and their future to make the cultural choices consciously and responsibly, to contribute to the palette of possibilities, and to generate the thoughts that we have so far been unable to think.

Remember, reading and writing are not literacy; they are the *tools* of literacy. Literacy itself is power. We feel both sadness and rage at the long-standing systemic problems in our society. How could we now, *now*, not all see the inequities in health care and law enforcement, economic and educational opportunities, job advancement? The COVID-19 pandemic asks us to put on one mask while it rips away so many others. And that has left us with a better understanding of other pandemics yet to be conquered: racism, homophobia, misogyny, child abuse, sex trafficking, and on and on. There are so many ills to heal, wrongs to right. A more responsible, more responsive, more compassionate, literate populace is a place to begin.

Aliya

So let's consider Aliya. She's a sixth grader who, with her book group, is reading *A Long Walk to Water* by Linda Sue Park. We talked with her about the book, and here's what she told us.

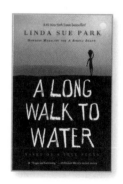

Aliya: This book made me so sad. I've never read a book like this.

Kylene: I agree. It's a hard book to read.

Aliya: Not really. It's right at my Lexile level.

Kylene: I didn't mean that. I mean that the ideas are tough. The experiences you're reading about are tough. Those children are living through horrifying times.

Aliya: I know. It makes me so sad. [pause] This really is a tough book. It's like tough in a different way. [pause] You know, books that make you really think. Why would people act that way? And when he had to leave that man who was dying of thirst? How do you decide to do that? I mean, what would I do? I think I'd save myself but what does that say about me?

Kylene: You're asking tough questions. Why do people act
             the way they do? [pause]

Aliya: I like this. Like really thinking about what I'd do.

Aliya is well on her way to becoming that more compassionate person our nation needs. She is open to feeling hurtful moments through literature and then stepping back to analyze her response to them. She's forging herself through her reading. The reading isn't shaping her, but the thoughts she is having in response to the reading certainly are.

Ben

Another student—his name long forgotten so we'll call him Ben—once told Kylene, "I know the book I'm reading is tough, but in a book, I can close it and walk away if it gets too hard to handle. I can go back to it when I'm ready. In real life, you can't just walk away."

Again, we see that willingness to read tough texts, tough not because of syntax or vocabulary, but because of the truths about human nature they reveal. His life with an abusive father was one he could not talk about; but the character's life (thank you, Chris Crutcher) was just far enough removed that he could talk about that character, that character's anger, that character's fear, that character's decisions. Crutcher's book wasn't manipulating this young man; but it was showing him how someone else with a life similar to his felt his same emotions. Through the pages of that book, he felt empowered.

ZuZu

"I'm not going to sit here one more minute while you read this book aloud. Every time you say, 'n-word' in place of *that* word, you make me feel terrible. Did you ever even wonder how I was going to feel being the only Black person in the classroom while we read this book [*To Kill a Mockingbird*]? I'm tired of everyone staring at me."

And then that tenth grader got up, picked up her backpack, and walked out the door. The teacher stared at ZuZu as she walked out of the classroom. She told the class to keep reading silently and went after her. We sat at the back of the room where we had been. The students kept their eyes down and for about 20 minutes, no one turned a page. The bell rang. They left silently, and so did we.

While we don't know how that teacher fixed this wrong, we hoped that she didn't ignore it. What we saw was a strong young woman who was refusing to be disempowered any longer. We heard tough questions in her statement that we hoped would become the springboard for honest conversations in her classroom and perhaps in her school.

Sitting With Discomfort

If we are to sit with all the students like Aliya, like Ben, like ZuZu, like Lily, and if we are to bring Bishop, Kahneman, Wolf, and Harari into the classroom and treat reading as the opportunity to change, if we are to remember Wynton Marsalis's view that democracy requires empathy, then reading must be seen as an invitation to shape both self and society. When that is the case, we need to be prepared to deal with the difficult questions and the discomfort they might cause.

Yet, too often, we have not expected—perhaps not wanted—students to dare to raise the difficult questions. And when they have dared, too often we redirect conversations. We are discouraged when they ask, "When is this due?" or "Is it for a grade?" and yet, paradoxically, we don't encourage them to discuss the difficult questions that might lead to reexamination of values and beliefs. When we've heard questions such as the

> **❝Reading must be seen as an invitation to shape both self and society.❞**

ones that follow, far too often we've heard teachers push students to safer questions about plot development or comparison of characters. Why? Because as much as we may prefer discussions that encourage reflection, they often lead to uncomfortable discussions. There will be some who object to such conversations or others who want more focus on passing the test. We would argue that discomfort may be necessary if our goal is to help students think about significant issues, possibly change themselves, and perhaps even become activists who help others evolve and grow. Their responsible thought might lead to changes—in their classroom, school, place of worship, home, community—and might lead to a more just and equitable life for us all. Some such questions we've heard include:

- "Why do people act that way?" [after reading *The Watsons Go to Birmingham*]

- "If I were in a dangerous situation, would I save myself before someone else?" [after reading *A Long Walk to Water*]

- "Why are there so few books with people who look like me in my classroom?"

- "Why won't everyone stand up for the National Anthem?"

- "Why is history about Black people only about slavery?

- "If the Supreme Court says same-sex people can marry one another, why can't my prom date be the person I choose?"

- "Why do some people want Mexicans to be able to just come into the country and others don't?" [after reading *Mexican WhiteBoy*]

- "Why do we say we were here first when First Nations people were already here?"

When faced with these questions, too often we pivot to the standards, to the curriculum, to the script, and mumble, "Those are questions better discussed at home" because . . . because we do not know the answers, or worse, know the answers and don't want to admit them. Teachers have for too long been constrained by administrators who are themselves constrained by the well-dressed PTO chair who has explained, nicely, that "those types of questions just are not for school," or by the parent who posted on Facebook (September 2020), that the picture storybook *Ron's Big Mission* wasn't "the type of book to be read in second grade." It's the true story of astronaut Ron McNair who, at age nine, confronted the racist policy of his hometown library that wouldn't let Black people check out books. This principal, however, responded by reading the book to everyone (Kelly, 2020).

When Censorship Happens

Recently, a Black educator/writer/speaker/friend of ours was told by a school district's superintendent that during his (then) forthcoming virtual workshop with teachers, he could not say, "Black lives matter," "racist," or "antiracist." "Why?" he asked, far more calmly than we would have. The answer he received, closely paraphrased by us, was "Because those are issues our parents [mostly white] don't want schools to discuss." Our friend explained why this was not acceptable. His response convinced (or perhaps compelled) the superintendent to cease his efforts to censor the workshop.

But we wondered if we would have been given the same warning if we had been running that workshop, the presumption being that as white people we would not be talking about racism in this country. Would the superintendent have urged us to avoid sharing an antiracist agenda? Would he have presumed that racism would not be a topic we would address? There were so many levels of censorship to unpack. We're still unzipping all the suitcases.

Too many others do not have our friend's standing to say no to the restrictions they're handed. Too many teachers must walk that fine line between the dos and don'ts of their teaching and the tough questions that kids ask. Why are teachers so tired at the end of the day? Remember Kahneman? That complex thinking as you toe that fine line is tiring. Instead of arriving home (or turning off the screen) at the end of the day energized from the thinking your students have done, too often we know you arrive exhausted from the complex thinking you have done as you work to make everyone happy.

The answers to those tough questions cannot be found in a study guide, although studying issues they raise with books and colleagues will certainly help guide responses. Those responses require venturing into the unknown, even when that trip is unsettling; they require a disruption to our thinking; they require that we live for a while with discomfort, unease, and uncertainty. But reading—our texts, our lives, our world—can help us find and create answers.

So, What Do You Do?

When you choose to share tough texts, to have them on your shelves, to put them in your book clubs, to tell students about them, be honest with students. If talking to high schoolers about *Speak* by Laurie Halse Anderson, tell them it tackles the tough issue of rape; if reading *The Hate U Give* by Angie Thomas, tell them it tackles white police brutality against Black people. And don't be surprised at the complexity of the questions your students, even the younger ones, may raise.

While reading the picture book *The Other Side* by Jacqueline Woodson, two fourth-grade girls said they were surprised that the Black girl's mother wouldn't let her play with a white girl, but the Black girl's dolls were white. "Is this white privilege?" one asked.

> **❝When you choose to share tough texts, to have them on your shelves, to put them in your book clubs, to tell students about them, be honest with students.❞**

As another teacher read aloud *Enemy Pie* by Derek Munson, one smaller-than-average second grader sat on the carpet with his classmates listening intently, not participating in any of the turn-and-talk moments, only to raise his hand at the end and announce, "I don't have many friends. No one sits with me in the cafeteria. I was surprised that in this book it seemed so easy to get rid of enemies. Why do you think no one likes me? Do people just not like you when you are different?" His classmates sat stunned (and one of us sat crying, while the other stoically pretended not to tear up), and then two boys closest to him crawled over, put their arms around him, and said, "We'll be your lunch buddies."

In both classrooms, teachers told students to keep one simple question in mind, "What surprised you?" If someone tells you that the issues kids are raising are not addressing a standard, pick one. We're sure one of your district's standards is comparing and contrasting, about making text-to-self or text-to-text or text-to-world comparisons. And then let kids have the most important conversations about a text they ever could: how the text is helping them see themselves and the world differently.

9

From Hard Thinking to Hardly Thinking

CONSIDER THE FOLLOWING DATA:

- We use 56 million acres of land for animal agriculture and four million acres of land to grow produce.

- Seventy percent of grain in the U.S. is fed to farmed animals rather than to people.

- The world's cattle alone consumes a quantity of food equal to the caloric needs of 8.7 billion people—more than the entire human population on Earth.

- It takes 4,200 gallons of water per day to produce the food for a meat-eater's diet. It takes 300 gallons of water per day to produce the food for a person who eats a plant-based diet.

- One acre of land can produce 250 pounds of beef. That same acre of land can produce 50,000 pounds of tomatoes or 53,000 pounds of potatoes (Buff, 2017).

New Information Can Require New Thinking About Old Habits

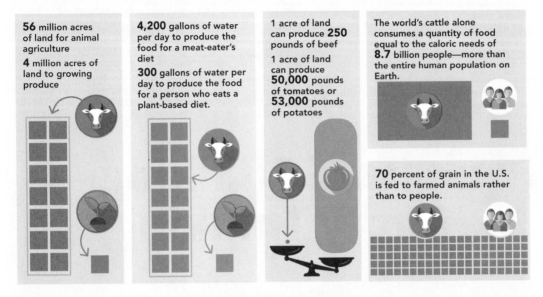

56 million acres of land for animal agriculture

4 million acres of land to growing produce

4,200 gallons of water per day to produce the food for a meat-eater's diet

300 gallons of water per day to produce the food for a person who eats a plant-based diet.

1 acre of land can produce **250** pounds of beef

1 acre of land can produce **50,000** pounds of tomatoes or **53,000** pounds of potatoes

The world's cattle alone consumes a quantity of food equal to the caloric needs of **8.7** billion people—more than the entire human population on Earth.

70 percent of grain in the U.S. is fed to farmed animals rather than to people.

(Buff, 2017)

In other words, we could go a long way in feeding the world and eliminating hunger in our nation and other places if we all adopted a plant-based diet rather than a meat-based diet. If you are not already a vegetarian or a vegan, which of the following would you be willing to do to solve world hunger:

- Become a full-time vegetarian.

- Give up meat, poultry, and pork at least three times a week.

- Give up meat, poultry, and pork at least once a week.

- None of those—I wouldn't change my diet.

What if making a change in your diet meant your parent or your child or your spouse or partner or dearest friend had a chance to live, to not starve to death? What if changing meant that someone you don't know and will never meet would not starve to death? What if that person lives in a village in a faraway country? Does your personal proximity to the problem make a difference in what you are willing to do to solve it? Is this getting hard to think about?

What if this isn't going to be about what you want to do, but is something that becomes a nationally or perhaps internationally mandated law? Now, we're talking about legally requiring a new lifestyle that (unless you are already a vegetarian) would limit your personal freedoms. Will you give up your burgers, your steaks, your chicken, and bacon?

And there are implications beyond what's for dinner tonight. We know—from the data above—that a meat-based diet requires more precious resources of land and water than a plant-based diet. But making this change to a plant-based diet will put thousands and thousands out of work as the meat/poultry/pork industries shut down. Other jobs will emerge, but the transition from cattle rancher to potato farmer, from meat packer to harvester, might not be easy or one that the cattle rancher or the meat packer wanted.

Now the decisions become harder. That's what new information does for us. How many of you are thinking, "I just don't want to figure that all out now," or "Well, maybe others could do that and I could continue eating what I want," or "This is too big of a problem for me to focus on now," or "I'd stop eating meat but my (fill in the blank) never would, so it wouldn't matter what I do," or "I just don't believe it. People have been eating meat since there have been people. If we weren't supposed to eat meat, then we just wouldn't be able to digest it."

"Now the decisions become harder. That's what new information does for us."

We've heard all these comments when we have shared these facts. And the most common response we receive: "I didn't know all that, but I really just don't think I could give up my meat."

Tough Thinking

Changing our minds is hard, especially when that change implies, perhaps demands, a lifestyle change. Ask anyone who has given up smoking, given up drinking, taken up jogging, reduced salt or eliminated it, taken up meditating, and so on. Change is hard. But at least those changes are encouraged and supported by science and stats. Change is harder when it requires us to examine our values, our long-held personal beliefs.

One couple we know has two adorable boys, who at this writing are still preschool age. But one is old enough to look around and notice that his family looks different from some of the other families he sees. His family has two moms. He knows he is loved and he knows he loves both his moms, but that didn't keep a little girl in the neighborhood park from wondering aloud to him one day why he has two moms. He shrugged and said, "I just do." She shrugged and replied, "Oh, okay," and they went back to playing. We love that story and wait impatiently for the day when more people, maybe all people, respond with such casual acceptance. Better yet, we wait for the day when no one even thinks to ask that question.

Both of those children are growing up in homes that are delivering the message that family is about love and commitment and respect. But we know that at some point, both will be confronted by children—perhaps they'll be teens by then—or adults who hold different views. Those less inclusive individuals probably will have been strongly influenced by their own families, communities, religious affiliations, and friends. Those less inclusive individuals may decide to use hurtful language, or the homophobia may be so ingrained in them by home or habit that it spews out without thinking, or they may try to hide it behind a genteel smile and an "Oh!" as the smile fades. In either case, their thinking will, in all likelihood, be immediate and without much consideration of its impact upon the listener or its implications about the speaker's own character.

Those reactions that diminish and dismiss, and perhaps condemn, some families will have probably been instilled since birth, and that may make it more difficult for people who have them to grapple with information that contradicts their assumptions, beliefs, and biases. Attitudes and thoughts that have been forged by affiliations—with families, religions, social groups within the school— are likely to be tenaciously defended. And that's one reason why it's hard to change minds.

> **66 Change is harder when it requires us to examine our values, our long-held personal beliefs. 99**

It's hard to change people's minds about a lot of things. Some topics are almost inconsequential: whether or not to cook cornbread in a cast iron skillet; whether you should clean the kitchen each night before bed or in the morning; whether you can open birthday presents before your birthday. Such things might make for family debates, but they really are of little consequence.

Other topics are more important, such as eating habits and the possible need to move from a meat-based diet to a plant-based diet. As of this writing, a critical topic is the wearing of masks to reduce the spread of COVID-19. Some say wearing a mask infringes on their personal freedom, and refuse to wear one. Others say that science, not opinion, reveals that wearing a mask helps slow the spread of the disease and will save tens of thousands of lives, so they wear one.

Likewise, there are parents who refuse to vaccinate their children, saying that it causes autism, although no reputable medical source supports that claim. Then there are people who, no matter the evidence from scientists, say with much conviction, "I just don't believe in climate change," or "I don't believe in evolution," even though "belief" is, of course, utterly irrelevant in these cases.

There are those who think that the United States has always been "the land of the free" and choose to dismiss the early explorers' killing and plundering of the First Nations people. Racists can't be convinced they are racists; some people can't accept that women and men should earn equal pay for equal work. Some would deny the same rights to the LGBTQ community that they enjoy in the straight community. Why? Well, as one woman told us, nicely, with a smile and tug of her pearl necklace, "I just don't believe in gay people. I pray for them, you know, to be saved. But I don't believe in them."

Unsure exactly what she meant by "believe in them"—we guess she meant "approve of them"—and thinking gay people didn't need saving from anything except narrow-minded people, we didn't pursue the conversation. By introducing the concept of *belief,* she had declared that *thought* about this topic was off-limits. We calmed ourselves by muttering that believing neither brought something into existence nor condemned it to oblivion, and walked away. But teaching thinking is the business of schools. Teachers don't have the luxury of walking away.

And why does all this matter in a book about reading? Because this book is about creating readers who think, who live empowered lives, who live self-determined lives shaped by evidence and reason, vision and imagination. To get students to that point, we must recognize that it is hard to change our minds. Remember Kahneman from Chapter 2?

A Case in Point

A bat and a ball cost $1.10.

The bat costs one dollar more than the ball.

How much does the ball cost?

Here's a blank for you to write your answer: _____.

This text has, we are sure, a low Lexile level. But the thinking required to arrive at the right answer is more complex. Here is the conversation the two of us had as we discussed this problem:

Kylene: So, it's ten cents.

Bob: Nope.

Kylene: Sure it is. The bat costs one dollar more than the ball. Both cost one dollar and ten cents. So, the bat costs one dollar and that means the ball costs ten cents.

Bob:	Nope.
Kylene:	I'm pretty sure I'm right.
Bob:	I'm pretty sure you're not.
Kylene:	Okay. How much do you think the ball costs?
Bob:	Five cents.
Kylene:	That makes no sense. Where do you get five cents?
Bob:	You can't just look at the total cost and pick two numbers that add up to that. You have to compare the cost of each to the other. You have to confirm your result with the other parameter, which is the overall total of the two together.
Kylene:	I have no idea what you're talking about, Robert.[11]
Robert:	Let's go back to the beginning. The first parameter is that Object 2 costs the amount as Object 1 plus one dollar.
Kylene:	I don't think so.
Robert:	It's really quite simple. The ball costs five cents. The bat costs $1.05. The total is $1.10 and the difference between the two: $1.05 - $.05 is $1.00. Should I explain it again?
Kylene:	You should not.

From Kylene: Much of my thinking shut down during this conversation for two reasons. First, I discovered I really didn't give a damn about the cost of the ball or the bat or the bat and ball together. Second, though, I was embarrassed that I couldn't understand it as quickly

---

[11] Robert is what I call Bob when he makes me angry, as he did with his ability to understand this problem faster than I did. Of course, I was frustrated with myself but didn't want to admit to that... —KB

as Bob did. So, I dug in my heels. I didn't want to change my mind. Ego often gets in the way of changing our minds.

Once we can get our egos out of the way, then we have to return to the fact that one of us didn't care about the answer. The lack of relevance made the thinking too hard. Without relevance, rigor is simply hard.

Let's look at another example. Read the following poem. Take notes in the margin, draw a family tree, read it aloud, do whatever you need to do (short of hunting down Cliffs Notes on the Internet) to make it meaningful to you.

Letters to My Daughters #3

Your great-grandfather dreamed that his son
would be an engineer, the old man,
the blacksmith with square hands.
To the Finns up north in that snow country
engineer was like doctor today. In the forties
in Detroit, I learned to play the violin.
So did my father when he was a boy in Ishpeming.
He and I never spoke about becoming. Our conversation
was my bow slipping over the strings, my fingers
searching for notes to tell him, his foot tapping time.
That violin cracked ten years ago, it dried out
from loneliness in the coat closet,
Your grandfather, the engineer, sometimes plays his
at night behind a closed kitchen door.
Your grandmother sews and turns up the television.
But what of you two? The piano you practiced over
is still here, a deaf-mute in our living room.
I strike an imperfect chord now and remember
we never spoke of what was dreamed for you.

Some of you, we are sure, began reading quickly and then discovered your rate needed to slow. It wasn't that you couldn't decode words, though *Ishpeming* might have slowed you down.

It was probably that you became confused about who is related to whom and who is playing what instrument. Some of you may have skipped the title and when you went back, you had to reread with that in mind. You turned to rereading. A few of you might have sketched out a family tree. Some of you may be wondering who wrote it. Perhaps that would give you a clue.[12] And some of you likely gave up, hoping that once you got through it, we'd tell you what it means. Go ahead. Admit it. You looked at it. It was hard. So you just skimmed on through it.

What happened is that you were reading slowly, deliberately, carefully, and maybe that got tiresome. If something about this poem struck a chord with you (to borrow the music analogy from the poem), you might have stuck with it longer. If not, then perhaps the same way some of your students do, you decided to wait for the teacher to provide the meaning for you. It isn't that this poem is too hard for you to figure out; it's that some of you aren't interested enough in the poem to move to that slower thinking required to analyze it. A lot of people call that push to think harder "rigor." But as we said, rigor without relevance is simply hard.

When the Task Is Relevant

That said, our brains, at times, do like hard tasks.

We *like* the hard task when the task has relevance and meaning, and the results matter. When it has something to do with us, who we are, or who we are trying to become. Writing a book for us is not easy. But we like doing it; as a result, we're willing to stick with it.[13] And at times, we get so caught up in it, in the words, the thinking, and the excitement of the mosaic of thought created by Rosenblatt

---

[12] The poet is Judith Minty. We often leave off poet's names when sharing poems with students. They, too often, try to make poetry autobiographical. Since Judith is a woman, the narrator must be a woman. We'd rather they study the language to decide if the gender of the narrator is important to them.

[13] Or we were until yesterday. Enough is enough.

and Kahneman and Harari and Freire and Kendi and Bishop that it feels effortless. That's when we are in what Mihaly Csikszentmihalyi (1990) would call "flow." Flow is effortless concentration. It's not a lack of concentration—it's concentration that doesn't feel tiring. A race-car driver, making a turn at 150 mph, is concentrating hard, but that's a sport the driver loves, so the concentration is exhilarating rather than terrifying—as it would be for us. The surgeon performing a complicated transplant is concentrating very hard, but that concentration is exhilarating, energizing, and fulfilling. It's the focused thinking that is not draining because the surgeon is in the flow, as opposed to the quick, almost instinctive thinking that we do, for instance, when we see the stop sign. The kids spending hours trying to move from one level to the next on a complicated video game, trying again and again to get past one level without feeling the passage of time. Why? They are in the flow. It's that staying up late with a book you love, even as it demands that you work math problems you don't want to work! You're in the flow (or in a college class and this is required reading).

The student who loves physics—at any age—will smile at the problem to be solved. The pole vaulter who wants to get one-eighth

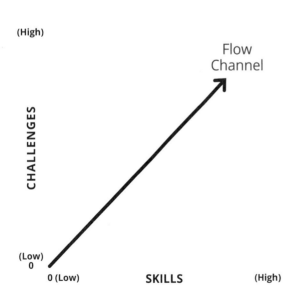

of an inch higher in her vault will work on technique long past sunset, requiring us to turn on the stadium lights. The student who desperately wants to understand what *Pet* by Akwaeke Emezi is all about, will reread the chapters until an "aha moment" arrives for her. Getting into the flow requires that the topic be personally motivating, be deeply engaging, be satisfying to the doer. Without that, the concentration is too taxing, and we're back to not caring what the bat and ball cost.

Relevance and Reading

And that's why relevance is so important.

At school, we work on trying to make topics interesting. But interesting is not the same as relevant. We find it interesting that in June 2020, a dust cloud that started in the Sahara Desert made its way to the southern United States, resulting in stunning sunrises and sunsets. But once the dust moved away from our horizons, that was it. We mentioned it as a topic of conversations during some dinners, but it didn't change the direction of our lives. For us, it was interesting. But for our friends who are environmental scientists, it mattered, and they are still talking about it. As in *still* talking about it. That event was very relevant to their work and their lives.

You see, relevance is about us. About you. Relevance is what matters to you. Or, when we are talking with students, it's about what matters to them. We think that much too often we don't capitalize on what is relevant to them and use that as the springboard to reading. And that's why choice is so critical when talking about reading (and writing). When kids get to choose what they read— not all the time but a good deal of it—they are more likely to choose what's relevant to them.

And with relevance, we're more likely to stick with a text, no matter its Lexile level, and consider tough issues. Maybe we're even open to changing our minds. And thus we grow. We are forged by our reading. And when that happens, we have the chance to change the world around us—whether that world is our home, our classroom, our neighborhood, or the world beyond. So, let's turn next to the issues kids tell us they want to address, the topics they want to read more about, the problems they want to solve.

10

Relevance: All That Really Matters

FROM KYLENE: IT WAS ONE OF THE MOST HORRIFYING moments in my teaching career. I was a second-year teacher. I had survived my first year and walked back into my middle school with far more confidence than I had any right to have. But in very early October, that confidence disappeared, immediately. Stephen took care of that.

Stephen was a seventh grader, smaller, shorter, and skinnier than most. Pale skin and jet-black hair with eyes that took in everything. He was quiet, rarely smiled, but wasn't sullen. He was there, but was contained, kept to his own accord, and didn't seem interested in seventh-grade silliness. He did what he was told, and I see now he was more compliant than engaged, but I was not smart enough then to know the difference.

That first week of October, I announced that for the next several weeks students would be studying what they wanted to study. I had no idea what I was doing, no idea what this meant. I was reacting to a concern that had festered since summer. I could not continue teaching via grammar packets (required by our department chair), in which students had to *master* prepositional phrases before they could move on to nouns. *Master* meant take three quizzes (already mimeographed for me), in which they would demonstrate with 90 percent proficiency that they could put parentheses around the prepositional phrases in 10 sentences. And then they could move on to nouns.

Stephen had not passed one quiz. And I had reached the point where I could no longer continue teaching that way. I decided that no matter the consequences I would face with my department chair, we were saying goodbye to packets and hello to personal questions. I announced to the class that they could pick a topic or an issue or a person—anything—and study that, and then we'd figure out how they would present their learning to the class. Stephen perked up. He literally sat up straight and for the first time that semester, he raised his hand to ask a question. He asked if I really meant *anything*. I nodded and then suddenly remembered I was teaching seventh graders and added, "Well, anything I approve of."

As the class ended and students turned in a list of topics or questions they wanted to research, most kids had several. Stephen had one: If you have cystic fibrosis and probably won't live past your mid-twenties, why do you have to go to school?

Stephen, his parents had decided, was old enough to keep his condition to himself, but not old enough to decide to drop out of school. I was horrified to realize that my student was critically ill, and I had not known. I was handing him packets to be completed when he was wondering how best to spend his expected shortened life. To this day, I ache when I think of that.

But once I knew, once I saw what mattered to him, I got out of the way. He began to write letters to the school board, to our local newspaper, to his doctors. He did research on the disease.

He began to tell his classmates of his illness. He explained the current treatment, and he spent time interviewing doctors throughout the nation to learn more. Our principal allowed him to make long-distance calls (at a time when mobile phones did not exist) to the Mayo Clinic and the Cleveland Clinic, so he could conduct interviews with specialists. He became involved in fundraising for cystic fibrosis at both local and national levels. He taught us all so much about living, and at times I have reflected on his lessons as I have fought my own battle with cancer.

And Stephen taught me that when something is relevant, nothing is too hard. And without relevance, no matter the Lexile level, it doesn't mean a thing. Not a damn thing.

The Tough Issues Kids Want to Consider

Kids want to make sense of things. They may not always want to make sense of the things we would like them to make sense of, but there is much that they want to understand.

66 ...without relevance, no matter the Lexile level, it doesn't mean a thing. Not a damn thing. 99

When we gathered information for our book *Disrupting Thinking*, we surveyed over a thousand students, asking them what big world problem they would like to help solve. We reported those findings in that book. For this book, we repeated the survey to see if responses had changed since 2017. Specifically, we asked, "What is one problem or issue (or maybe two) in the world, your city, your neighborhood, or your school you would really like to help solve?" The survey was up for only two days, and the number of participants was small (165), but we simply wanted to get a glimpse of the students' concerns. The responses ranged widely.

One student said quite simply and without any explanation, "Lyme disease." Why that was his major concern, we have no idea. Perhaps he or someone he knew suffered from it. Perhaps he had some reason to be especially afraid of it. He knew enough about the disease to spell it properly, so that indicated some familiarity with the problem, but beyond that it remains a mystery. We think of him occasionally, wondering if he had Lyme disease, how he's doing, if he's growing up to become a doctor, and what his concerns are now.

We think, too, of the young man who reported, "There is a poor process to connect live buglers with military families needing a bugler at a funeral." It was a concern that we hadn't anticipated, but we can see that if you need a live bugler and can't find one, then you do have a problem to solve.[14] And if that problem struck close to home, then it was probably a serious issue for the young man. We hoped that he found one and have wished to this day that we knew how it all turned out. Perhaps some thoughtful teacher helped direct him in an Internet search that might have taken him to the site we found or one similar.

Yet another student articulated his concern somewhat more fully:

> A problem that is very dear to me in the world is African Americans being treated differently because of their race. And how people think we are so violent and dangerous because we may be darker than a Caucasian person. And how we can be walking on the street and get pulled over by a racist police officer and be put to the ground or shot down because we were "resisting arrest" and then when we choose to fight for our race by peacefully protesting against racism and then social media decided to put a dangerous label on us when we just want to be treated equally.

This ninth grader was concerned with the issue that has been plaguing this country since its inception. It's the issue that is now being addressed every day in the media, the concern that is driving

---

[14] Subsequent research, in the days after first reviewing the results of the survey, led us to an organization that would have helped—https://www.buglesacrossamerica.org—but by then we had no way of getting in touch with the student.

Topics Kids Say They Want to Learn About

- COVID-19
- Racism
- Pollution
- Hunger
- Bullying
- Police Brutality
- Violence
- Global Warming
- Poverty
- Sexism

people to march, the passion that is motivating people in even such a distant place as England to tear down and toss into the harbor the statue of the slave trader Edward Colston (McGreevy, 2020), and the problem that has led a conservative organization such as NASCAR to ban Confederate flags from its events because of their association with the racism that this young man was worrying about (Roots, 2020).

Very few of the concerns the students expressed might be seen as trivial or uniquely personal. (Although one seven-year-old wondered how to convince his mom that carrots are not a valuable vegetable.) Most of them, like the one about racism, echoed the concerns of thoughtful adults. Another student was concerned with the quality and quantity of food on the school's lunch menu—this fourth grader may grow up still interested in world hunger, nutrition, or a cure for diabetes. These early interests, if we embrace them and respect them, can become shaping influences in later life choices. What impressed us the most was that their responses were similar to those we heard from the 1,000-plus students in the survey for *Disrupting Thinking*.

As you look at the chart on the left, and remember this is what kids say is important to them, ask yourself how your students are given the opportunity to explore those interests.

Except for COVID-19, these were the same topics students mentioned in early 2017. The addition of COVID-19 shows how responsive our students are to current events, even our youngest students. Kylene's five-year-old friend told her she wanted to do two things: solve how to get "knots out of hair" and "fix it so no one is sick so we can all go play with one another."

These are not insignificant, trivial, private, merely personal issues (except the distaste for carrots, perhaps)—they are the issues of contemporary American society. They are in the national news, often the headlines, almost every day. The problems these kids would like to help solve are the very problems we are trying desperately, as a society, to solve.

From Their Mouths

We think the students' comments are valuable enough for you to read through more of them.

High School Students

- Coronavirus and murder hornets.

- There's a lot of violence. People don't get to use their voices as much as they should be allowed to.

- I feel as though racism, police brutality, and all the riots that have been happening these days are a major problem in the world.

- All the violence, world hunger, injustice, and police brutality.

- One problem or issue in the world that I would really like to solve is human rights. Everybody should have freedom, freedom of speech, and the right to an education or work regardless of gender, race, language, ethnicity, or religion. Everyone is entitled to be treated equally without discrimination.

- The intense judgment that people possess. I hate feeling judged or seeing others be judged just because of their skin color, sexuality, or past.

Middle School Students

- People around the world are going hungry and that's not okay, especially because so many of us in countries like America have the money and privilege to stop it. We should also focus on BLM, because it's such a huge problem in America.

- One problem in the world right now in my opinion is that a lot of parents do not know how to have fun. They are always working, and they don't realize that they are just working to get food, and they are just eating food to live. And they are just living to work. So, there is no fun in their life.

- Child labor in Africa where they have to work in the mines that kill thousands of innocent kids every year. It is wrong and just pure evil to make kids work at eight years old with no pay, no safety, and not letting them go to school.

- Pollution, I want so bad to rid the world of harmful substances that are harming the air, water, people, animals, and Earth itself.

- There is a problem in the way we politically categorize race. Just because you are a certain race doesn't mean you think one way or another, this very idea is racist (stereotyping). As a white male, my first friends were a family of Somali Americans that lived next door (at the time). We were a different race, religion, culture, you name it! I don't want to inherit a world that delegitimizes my opinions and capabilities based upon my sex and race. Just as the great Martin Luther King, Jr., dreamed of a color-blind society, so do I.

- I know it seems like something small, but this is something I'm really passionate about. I feel like 70 percent of dog owners shouldn't have dogs because of their lack of knowledge. There are many reasons but here are just a few: people keep getting a specific dog breed because they saw a professionally trained one on TV and think that it's going to be the perfect dog; many also don't want to spend the money or time training the dog which then creates a liability wherever the dog goes because it can be reactive; and the last reason is one that angers me very much—unfortunately obese dogs are becoming "cute" and "chonky" among pet owners and then they call fit dogs "abused."

- Drug use, I see at least 20 people every day stop at the parks in my neighborhood to go in the woods and smoke or vape or stuff like that. Most are teenagers that are being stupid.

Elementary School Students

- Two issues in the world I want solve are deforestation and laws in several states in the U.S. against same-sex marriages. [Yes, we checked. This is a fifth-grader's response.]

- We should pay each other fairly and we shouldn't give one person more because that person gave us some good treats or whatever. You should pay each other equally.

- I would like to help solve the issue with COVID-19 spreading.

- I want to figure out why people do not like people.

Students Want to Work on Big Problems

Our 2020 survey of K–12 students reveals they want to help solve big problems. More than 50% said that they were ready to take on the work right now.

I've never thought about whether or not I could help solve big problems.

I think I could help solve big problems now.

I think that kids should wait until they are adults to work on big problems.

Literature, Our Way In

Some of those responses are also the very issues that lie at the heart of much of the literature that we teach. The issue of bullying, for instance, is addressed in picture books for young children (*My Name Is Bilal, Enemy Pie, My Hair Is a Garden, Chrysanthemum*) and in young adult novels (*The Chocolate War, Some Girls Are, Thirteen Reasons Why*). Racism is addressed in the picture storybook *The Other Side* and in novels, such as *All American Boys* or *Dreamland Burning*. Other titles that align with students' concerns are easy to find through countless websites[15]—there is no need to list titles here because checking one or two of these sites will bring you right up to date.

In other words, respecting the students' interests need not take us too far afield from what we are obligated to teach. We don't have to abandon the teaching of literature in order to respond to the interests of the students. In fact, the interests of the students and those of the writers we might like to teach are very much in line with one another. Shakespeare, writing *Romeo and Juliet*, was interested in the conflict that arises between two groups—families—within a community; Sharon Draper, writing *Romiette and Julio,* was interested in the same issue in another time and another place—in this case the conflict of interracial dating; much of the current fiction for children and young adults is about conflicts: race, religion, ethnicity, class, gender. Your students are almost certainly concerned with the same issues. The conflict may seem minor to us—perhaps the chafing between the athletes and the intellectuals—or major—racial conflicts that have the potential for erupting into violence. But if there are conflicts, we may be certain that, whatever they may be, they are of great concern to the students involved in them.

---

[15] These will get you started:
- www.readbrightly.com
- www.goodreads.com
- diversebooks.org
- www.whatdowedoallday.com/books-for-kids
- www.ala.org
- booklists.yalsa.net

The literature may be a way of dealing with the conflict or other issues, without demanding that students make themselves too vulnerable to the scrutiny of their classmates. Remember Ben, from Chapter 8? As he read one of Chris Crutcher's books, he could reflect upon and write about the situation with a level of detachment. These problems were the character's problems, and yet he could find solace in seeing a character deal with his same situation. Remember the second grader who read *Enemy Pie* and asked why he didn't have friends? Literature opens doors.

Thus, the students might discuss the thinking of the characters, the interactions of the groups, the consequences of actions for the individuals and the community, and gradually, as they grow comfortable with the topics, introduce into the conversation as much of their personal lives as they feel comfortable sharing. No student should feel that he has to be exposed, or that he has to represent a group to which he belongs. The student who said, on the survey, "If someone does something about a bully after telling you, don't get angry at them, they told you about the bully and you sat on your hands about it," shouldn't feel that he has to tell his story, or that he has to represent victims or friends of victims. We might worry about the implied threat of revenge, but that's another issue. The student, however, might have important contributions to make in the discussion of any books that feature a vulnerable individual victimized by a stronger one or by a group.

And as that student deals with the issue, through the reading of significant texts, the conversation with other students and the teacher, and writing, the student may be rethinking his own values and conceptions, his own way of seeing the world. With luck, the work of the classroom might lead the students to reshape their understanding of the conflicts in which they are engaged, perhaps coming to understand them more thoroughly, perhaps seeing them through the eyes of others, including the people with whom they have come in conflict, and perhaps changing—if only slightly— the ways in which they work through those conflicts.

The more powerful possibility for the classroom, however, may lie not simply in the connections to be had with the literature students read, not just in the relevance our students may be invited to find there, but in the possibility that students could attack the problems of bullying, of racial conflict, of the oppression or abuse of individuals whose gender identity doesn't match the gender they were assigned at birth, or of any other major issue that students are interested in. Mehta and Fine (2019) speak of school environments in which learning started with a purpose—something that was not preparation for later life but could grab the interest of a young person in the present. Students were treated as producers; that is, as people who could offer interpretations, solve problems, develop products of value, and otherwise create in ways consistent with the norms of the field or discipline. Subjects were treated as open-ended rather than closed; there was a belief that what students were discovering or creating had significant value, not that knowledge had been previously discovered and needed only to be transmitted (p. 364).

Reading the Immediate Importance

In such an environment as that, the students were doing more than simply preparing for something to come after graduation. They weren't reading to check off another standard to show it had been covered. They were beginning to work on their own on the matters that concern them. Relevance, for them, was not just a matter of passing interest. Rather, it was a matter of immediate importance. The work they were doing was shaping their lives, creating the conceptual world in which they would live. They would be forming their values, taking in and making sense of information, deciding whom they trusted and what they would think. They cannot avoid doing that. Getting through the day demands it. Their very survival depends upon it. But now, in this school, they would be doing it collaboratively with other students, with the teacher, with the great writers who have contributed to the thinking about significant issues, with the characters those writers have invented. Far better that they make sense of the world in those circumstances than alone or in the gangs, groups, and cliques that chance may offer them.

And that seems to be what students want to do. They want what they do to be significant now, not simply preparation for doing something that may be significant later. Of the students that we surveyed, most said both that they would like to help address the issues that were important to them now and that they thought they *could* help now, even while still young, still in school. Over half of them said that they think they can help solve big problems, problems like the ones they shared.

> **"They want what they do to be significant now, not simply preparation for doing something that may be significant later."**

The point is that these students want to be involved. They want to focus on significant issues. They want to be doing something that matters instead of simply preparing for the future when the schools have graduated them and certified that they are ready to participate. Some sadly reported that they didn't think they could do much. One said, in a voice that we imagined quiet, resigned, depressed, "I can't really solve anything," but many shared the more aggressive and optimistic attitude of those students who have stepped out of their assigned roles and done something.

Our students have concerns that can enrich their interactions with our subject matter and with us. Those concerns may make the school experience more relevant and effective. Many students have already struck out on their own or with the assistance of teachers.

Unfortunately, but not surprisingly, not all of their concerns were quite as significant as those we've been discussing. One young man lamented, "We didn't get to do any of the fun stuff we were supposed to this year for school, and I am super bored." It may take more digging to find out what issues—what larger issues—matter to him.

Finally, one student, perhaps knowing that the survey might someday find its way into the hands of teachers, both identified and exemplified the problem he wished to solve. He wanted "to help the schools have better edication."

"But, Bob and Kylene,
We Have Standards to Cover"

Yes, you do.

But they are too low. Our school standards, while detailed, precise, and, yes, often hard to meet, are too low. They have gotten us to where we are today—mostly a nation that chooses not to read; mostly a nation that hits "share" on the social media platform without checking the truth of a statement; mostly a nation that has replaced the hard work of thinking with the easier task (if it can be called that) of believing; mostly a nation that still does not live up to its ideals of equality and democracy.

> 66 **But for most teachers, for you, school is about deep learning; about questioning; about discovering; and perhaps most joyfully, school is about hope.** 99

When Greta Thunberg, the teen activist from Sweden, was asked on Trevor Noah's *The Daily Show* (September, 11, 2019) how she would explain the difference in what Americans have to say about climate change and what Swedes would say, she paused, reflected, and then explained that in the U.S. we are still talking about whether we believe in climate change. In Sweden it's not about believing or not believing. It's a fact.

Yes, we are a nation that defaults to what we believe too often. We didn't go far enough in *Disrupting Thinking*. We should have said to stop everything and first rethink why we go to school. For some adults, who are mostly policymakers, school means daycare; for others, it's a way to show we're ahead (in what we're not sure) when compared to other countries; for still others, it's about proving that kids can perform certain academic tasks at certain levels. But for most teachers, for you, school is about deep learning; about questioning; about discovering; and perhaps most joyfully, school is about hope. Hope walks through the classroom door each day, and teachers look up and smile. It's time we reclaim those reasons for schooling because what we've been doing didn't work.

11

"So What?"

SO, YOU HAVE HOPE. OKAY. IF YOU'RE A PRAGMATIST
as we are, you probably wonder, so what? How do I help reading
empower kids? After all, reading only empowers if we let it.

In *Disrupting Thinking*, we quoted a student who said, "You read
it and so what?" We don't think we realized, at the moment, how
important a question that was. He was ready to take on the harder
thinking about whether that reading meant something to him.
Had we grasped what he was doing, we would have seized upon it
immediately, asked the student his name so that we could thereafter
properly credit him, hoisted him onto our shoulders, and marched
off to the principal's office to celebrate his brilliance.

The Value of "So What?"

Neither the student nor we understood the importance of this
question. As we listened carefully, we heard his litany of complaints.
The chart below shows what he *actually* said and what, by listening to
his intent and not just his words, we understood:

What the Student Said	What We Understood
"I hate boring books."	He is tired of reading what does not matter to him.
"I hate answering dumb questions."	He is frustrated with needing to answer someone else's questions about a text.
"You come into class and you have to copy down on your daily sheet the day's standard that is on the board. Bo-ring."	He doesn't see a relationship between his life, his curiosities, and standards that have been imposed upon him.
"I hate having to write a response to everything I read in my response journal. I'm like, 'I liked it,' but then I get a 'Tell me more.' Bo-ring."	He is tired of writing assignments that are ritualistic. Always having to write a response after reading can, for some, turn reading into an experience that's more about finishing an assignment than enjoying the text.
"I hate having to read purple dot books. My friends are reading the I Survived books. Why can't I?"	Reading, a solitary act, is actually a social experience. He wants to read what his buddies are reading so he can join their conversations about those books. We don't know if the I Survived books have a dot with a color that indicates they are more or less complex—vocabulary, syntax, need for prior knowledge—than purple-dotted books. And we don't really care. If we want motivated kids, then sometimes we have to let them read what motivates them.
"You read it and so what?"	Reading has become an exercise for him. It has nothing to do with him or for him. It is a school-based experience.

You, too, probably hear similar comments from some of your students. "I hate reading." "Why do I have to read this?" "Why can't I read what I want?" "Why do we have to keep a journal?" We encourage you to do what we do and think carefully about what else is being asked or said beyond the surface statement. Make a chart, as we did. Talk with colleagues. Ask each other, "What's behind this statement?"

Hearing the Unsaid

If you do want to empower readers, if you want to pivot from what hasn't been working toward something that might work better, then the first thing we'd suggest you do is learn to listen, truly listen. Lean in and hear what a particular student is telling you. We know, we've just suggested what is easy to say and hard to do. If you are a middle school or high school teacher with 120 students or more, you might be tempted to stop reading now. Please don't. We also recognize this is very hard with "only 60" students, and for those of you with the wiggling, call-on-me-hands-waving-in-the-air classroom of a "mere" 22, that number can be the hardest. We know this idea of knowing all your students, especially if you see them for a mere 45 minutes a day, seems unreasonable at best, impossible at worst. And how do you lean in to listen when a screen separates you and a child? We do ask of you the near impossible, we know.

What's our answer? Start with the reasonable. Begin with the possible. Identify quickly which students need you the most. In the upper grades, they are usually the ones who push you away the fastest. Those shrugged shoulders and mumbled "I dunno" answers, that swagger in the walk and brag in the talk, that step back as you step forward, which can mean *I've given up on thinking you can help* and, tragically, sometimes means *I don't think I can be helped.* Start there. Start with those kids.

We think policy-makers, parents, some principals, and some super-teachers often have unrealistic expectations that you can plan, differentiate, assess, work with colleagues, attend faculty meetings, read memos, redo lesson plans based on unexpected events of the day, learn standards, forget those standards to learn new standards, AND get to know, personally and deeply, each teen, each child you teach each day. Those with such unrealistic expectations have not walked in your shoes. Or even stood at the back of your classroom. Should the goal be to know all your kids? Of course. But sometimes, *we know*, there are some kids we just never get to know as well as we want. And sometimes our own lives interfere. Aging parents need our help. Children get sick—sometimes tragically ill. Marriages arrive and some dissolve. Trips to the orthodontist or veterinarian or a church meeting or the grocery store or doing the laundry or visiting a friend—all take time.

Sometimes, when class sizes grow beyond the reasonably manageable, knowing all your kids well is not possible. Ask yourself this—or perhaps ask your principal: Has any doctor ever seen 120 patients in a day? Does a plumber get to 120 houses in a day? Does a hair stylist see 120 clients in a day? No. When faced with the near impossible, ask yourself:

- Which kids do I need to know best and first?
- Is there a child/teen who appears to need immediate attention today?
- Who is hiding behind silence or hiding behind unexpected behavior?
- Whom have I managed to not see?
- Whose voice has been missing?

Then, when you lean in and listen to those kids, you'll begin to hear them—especially the silent ones. When a missing one returns, greet him or her with "I missed you" rather than "Here's your work to make up." When you sit near a silent one and ask, "What's wrong?" the answer "Nothin'" rarely (never?) means *nothing*. But compare that answer to a student's bare shake of the head before walking away. The latter says, "I don't trust my voice to say anything." The former says, "I don't yet trust you to share." And both of those are different from the message of the kid who stands there, hands in pockets or folded across the chest, and answers that question with a shrug—but stays standing there, eyes darting from the desk to you from time to time. Learning to listen is hard. But we don't know what to do with "I read it and so what?" until we really hear what the student is saying.

> **But too often we miss opportunities to empower because the voice that's heard the loudest in the classroom is our own.**

In a book about reading, why are we talking about listening to students' language? Because it is through language—written and oral—that students' identities, empowerment, and independence can begin to emerge. But too often we miss opportunities to empower because the voice that's heard the loudest in the classroom is our own.

To help us focus on students' voices, we sometimes use a chart like the one you'll see on pages 112–113. The first column is where we jot a comment from a student. The second column is where we write what the student probably meant. The third column offers you ideas for addressing the concern. We've provided a completed chart using student comments you might hear.

What the Student Said	What We Needed to Hear	What's Our "So What?"
"I hate boring books."	He is tired of reading what does not matter to him.	Check your books. Are they inclusive so that students can see themselves and see far beyond themselves? Have you asked students what big problems they want to solve? We've discovered asking, "What interests you?" often encourages "I dunno" as an answer. So, we now ask, "Is there a big problem—at our school or in the world you'd like to solve?" That almost always gets detailed answers.
"I hate answering dumb questions."	He is frustrated with needing to answer someone else's questions about a text.	Teacher questions—even the best ones—are teacher questions. Start with the Three Big Questions, and that will usually lead them to asking more and more questions of their own.
"You come into class and you have to copy down on your daily sheet the day's standard that is on the board. Bo-ring."	He doesn't see a relationship between his life, his curiosities, and standards that have been imposed upon him.	If this is a building requirement, then until you can have the conversations that perhaps change that, you have to follow through. But perhaps you move it to the end of class and you ask, "How did what we did today connect to the idea of seeing how authors develop characters?"
"I hate having to write a response to everything I read in my response journal. I'm like, 'I liked it,' but then I get a 'Tell me more.' Bo-ring."	He is tired of writing assignments that are ritualistic. Always having to write a response after reading can, for some, turn reading into an experience that's more about finishing an assignment than enjoying the text.	Unless you write a response in your journal every time you read something, stop doing this. Using ideas from reading to help spur ideas for writing is smart. Routinized journal responses can be tiring. Ask him how he wants to think about the ideas he's gathering as he's reading.

"I hate having to read purple dot books. My friends are reading the *I Survived* books. Why can't I?"

Reading, a solitary act, is actually a social experience. He wants to read what his buddies are reading so he can join their conversations about those books. We don't know if the *I Survived* books have a dot with a color that indicates they are more or less complex—vocabulary, syntax, need for prior knowledge—than purple-dotted books. And we don't really care. If we want motivated kids, then sometimes we have to let them read what motivates them.

Review with faculty the research on whether reading leveled texts actually improves higher-level comprehension and deepens engagement. If you do use leveled texts during the instructional time, make sure kids don't confuse that reading with independent reading. The use of leveled texts might be appropriate for guided reading/small-group instruction for a small portion of the school day.

"You read it and so what?"

Reading has become an exercise for him. It has nothing to do with him or for him. It is a school-based experience only.

Have talks with colleagues in your school about your mission statement for reading. Not the standards, but why in your school you want kids to become engaged, independent, skillful readers. Check to see if your thinking involves the creating of empowered readers. Ask what it was that turned you into a reader? A special diorama you made in sixth grade? Drawing a new front cover? Rewriting the final chapter so it ends a different way? What is your "So what?" about what you read? Students are probably looking for the same.

12

Leaning In

WHAT FOLLOWS IS A TRANSCRIPT FROM A FOUR-minute discussion that five eighth graders had after reading—on their own—"Thank You, M'am" by Langston Hughes.[16]

If you've been in a workshop with us, then you've probably seen the video of the students having this conversation and can picture them. If not, look at the photos on the following page. The first three photos show the five students who are the discussants in this transcript. The fourth one shows you where we were during this conversation. As you can see, we were at the back of the room, with one of us blowing her nose.[17]

---

[16] This is a short story about a 14-year-old boy who tries to steal a woman's purse. She seizes him, but rather than haul him off to the police, she takes him to her apartment, feeds him, gives him the money he wanted, and then sends him on his way. He has learned a lesson but is unable to express his thanks.

[17] This is, without doubt, one of my most unflattering photos ever. I'm hoping, though, that all of you have at some point stood at the back of the room and blown your nose. It does prove, however, that we weren't sitting with the students, encouraging their talk. That said, every time I see this photo, that's exactly where I wish I had been. Sigh. —KB

Top (left to right): Shania, Lauren, Tanisha, Darian
Bottom: Marcus

This transcript picks up after they've said some introductory things, such as "This was good" or "I liked it" or "Did you hear what so and so said about so and so . . . ." Eventually, they settled down and began discussing the text. They had one prompt to guide their thinking: "What surprised you?" We begin with Lauren talking about what would happen today if someone tried to steal your purse, the opening event of this short story.

We're going to ask you to read this two times. This first time, just enjoy their conversation. And please be patient with the occasional mazes the students stumble into, as we all do from time to time in oral language.

Lauren: You'd think that people, they may be mad because they try to take your pocketbook, which he tried to take her purse and people may be mad. They wouldn't just take him in, give him 10 dollars, wash them, clean them, and feed them.

Darian: Well, nowadays people won't be so considerate and they figure, okay, he stole my pocketbook. He tried to steal from me. So why should I try to be nice to him? Or they try to lock you up or even try to kill you nowadays, but she did something different. That's why this passage surprised me when I saw it, because they act in a different way than real life would now.

Lauren: Yeah, that's what I think because it's like nothing I've ever seen in my life. That's why it shocked me when we read it. Because you would be like, well maybe we would be like, just let him go. Like maybe some think like if he's out on the street, what makes you think you have to take him in as your own son that he's gonna be good? And I wonder why he didn't run when he had the chance. Like why he'd stay there if he felt so bad, like . . .

Tanisha: He was like probably because he probably didn't have a family, but he tried to run the whole time.

Lauren: All right. But he was trying to run the whole time. He was like, just let me go. She's like, are you hungry? You like? No, like, he didn't want the help. And then he got there and didn't tried to run. I wonder why he didn't.

Tanisha: He probably did that because he didn't have any money. Probably didn't have a family. That's why he snatched her purse to start with.

Shania : I want to know why he tried to take her pocketbook only to get some money for some shoes. I want to know, what was so special about the shoes that he wanted them so bad? Was it that other kids that he thought was better than him had it so he thought he had to have them? Or I wonder, like, what was his family at? Why wasn't they there when he needed things? Why was he out at night? Because it was dark. And why would you try to snatch somebody's purse?

You shouldn't do something to somebody else's family that you wouldn't want nobody to do to yours. You have to think about it because like, if you do that, if I do something you or somebody do something to somebody else. You got to think about what is that person doing to my family? And you wouldn't like that. So I don't understand why he would do that.

Darian: Maybe he wanted them shoes because he never had some. Maybe he never had a pair of new shoes. Maybe when he had a family, he always had his brother's old shoes. Maybe he wanted some new shoes.

Lauren: Oh, maybe something handed down or he just wants something to make him feel like popular for like one day at least. She still gave him the money. I think she was real considerate about him.

Shania: But you have to think about it. Do he have a family? Do he have a brother? Do—does he have a mom? Does he live with his mom or dad?

Darian: He had to have a family to get here some way. He had to have a mom and dad for him to exist.

Lauren: I still wonder why she took him in. Because just because somebody doesn't have somebody you see a lot of poor people in this street outside. But that doesn't mean I'm going to go run over and take him in my house. I wonder what was so good about him that she took him in?

Darian: She cares so much about his appearance.

Lauren: Right.

Shania: Maybe she had a son, but something happened to her son. And she just feel like, you know, she just took him in, at that point of time and just try to like show him right from wrong. Just from there. And maybe to teach him like he shouldn't be, shouldn't be trying to take people's stuff like that. It's still in his wrong.

Tanisha: She probably thought that he may have felt she was trying to be like a mom. If she lost her son or she had a son before that, she was going to be like another mom trying to kind of make him feel at home. Like that was her son.

Marcus: I think that I think that she gave him the 10 dollars, because when she was little, she tried to snatch people's pocketbooks, too.

Darian: Maybe she grew up the same way and shame on him and end up being like her.

Lauren: I think maybe she could've had a bad past.

Darian: And she is like, I don't want you to be the same way that I was. She want him to be better than she was.

Shania: But she did say that she did do something in her life that was wrong because she said it like she said she wasn't going to tell him, because [she said] I wouldn't tell nobody what I did in my lifetime if I'm trying to teach you a lesson. If it was bad. . . .

What we hope you'll do now is return to the transcript and mark the parts that show you these students are answering the prompt "What surprised you?," are empowered readers, and are taking charge of their own thinking and their own learning. You might mark sections or lines that illustrate to you their ability to listen to others, to speculate, to use text evidence, to make inferences, and to draw tentative conclusions.

Now that you've marked your text, compare your analysis with a colleague's. In particular, we'd suggest that you consider what you've seen with your district standards in mind. What standards have been addressed in this conversation?

Once you've done that, read on for our observations. Or, if you're doing this after school at a restaurant, have more nachos. And a(nother) margarita.

Our Analysis of This Conversation

We find several aspects of this conversation intriguing. The first is that students do respond to the prompt and do conduct the discussion entirely on their own. There is no teacher intervening, there are no questions coming from the front of the class, and no judgments are passed on the speculations and answers of the group. They raise the questions themselves, trade their perspectives back and forth, and build on what the previous speaker has said. It begins with an observation about the unexpected actions of Mrs. Luella Bates Washington Jones, the woman accosted by 14-year-old Roger:

> You'd think that people, they may be mad because they try to take your pocketbook, which he tried to take her purse and people may be mad. They wouldn't just take him in, give him 10 dollars, wash them, clean them, and feed them.

Lauren observes that Mrs. Jones is behaving in a way she thinks unlikely. If someone tries to steal your purse, she says, you wouldn't give him money and take him into your home.

Darian concurs, pointing out in more detail that Mrs. Jones is not behaving as we think most people might today:

> Well, nowadays people won't be so considerate and they figure, okay, he stole my pocketbook. He tried to steal

from me. So why should I try to be nice to him? Or they try to lock you up or even try to kill you nowadays, but she did something different. That's why this passage surprised me when I saw it, because they act in a different way than real life would now.

"This passage surprised me," he reports. These students have been reading with the Three Big Questions (see page 133) in mind for the school year, so we were not surprised to hear Darian say this, but we were heartened. He's contrasting what Mrs. Jones did with what he thinks "real life" would be like. So, if "compare and contrast the actions of a character with another character or a real person" is one of your standards, mark Darian as "can do."

Both Lauren and Darian were stating and beginning to explore their own perceptions of the text. Darian compares the behavior of Mrs. Jones to what someone "today" might do. He asks why she should be nice to Roger since he tried to steal from her and says that people "try to lock you up or even try to kill you nowadays." The character, he says, is acting in a way that's different from what he would expect to see on the streets today.

Darian wasn't responding to the request that he make a text-to-world connection. That's a critical connection to make, and it is certainly a type of connection we want readers to make. We happen to think, however, that this type of connection rarely occurs on demand. When was the last time you sat down with a good book and reminded yourself that yesterday you made two text-to-text connections, so this evening you should focus on text-to-world connections? As critically important as it is to remember that there are many ways to connect with a text, we think it is better when those connections occur naturally. Then, if you need to use that language with students, say something like, "As I was wandering around the room, I heard Darian make an important text-to-world connection. He said . . . ."

Again, what seems significant to us is that the issue arose from the student's observations and not from the teacher's interrogations or demands. The students gave some thought to what surprised them in the text and compared the text to what they would have expected from the people they might encounter in "real life."

They have, in other words, brought their own experiences to the text and used them to try to understand it. In the next, rather long, statement by Shania, other questions emerge:

> I want to know why he tried to take her pocketbook only to get some money for some shoes. I want to know, what was so special about the shoes that he wanted them so bad? Was it that other kids that he thought was better than him had it so he thought he had to have them? Or I wonder, like, what was his family at? Why wasn't they there when he needed things? Why was he out at night? Because it was dark. And why would you try to snatch somebody's purse? You shouldn't do something to somebody else's family that you wouldn't want nobody to do to yours. You have to think about it because like, if you do that, if I do something to you or somebody do something to somebody else. You got to think about what is that person doing to my family? And you wouldn't like that. So I don't understand why he would do that.

Shania wonders and speculates:

- What makes Mrs. Jones think she has to take him in?
- What makes her think that he's going to be good?
- Why didn't he run when he had the chance?
- Maybe he didn't run because he didn't have any money.
- Maybe he didn't have a family.

If you have any standards to cover that include requiring that students will question the text, make speculations, draw conclusions, or make inferences, you can mark Shania "done" for all of those. She offers her questions, not ours. She shows confidence—not the confidence of being right, but the confidence of freedom to wonder. Once we recognize that discussions aren't to show what students know but are to show what they are coming to know, then learning shifts.

We want you to reread Shania's words. This time, mark the lines that reveal her confidence:

> I want to know why he tried to take her pocketbook only to get some money for some shoes. I want to know, what was so special about the shoes that he wanted them so bad? Was it that other kids that he thought was better than him had it so he thought he had to have them? Or I wonder, like, what was his family at? Why wasn't they there when he needed things? Why was he out at night? Because it was dark. And why would you try to snatch somebody's purse? You shouldn't do something to somebody else's family that you wouldn't want nobody to do to yours. You have to think about it because like, if you do that, if I do something to you or somebody do something to somebody else. You got to think about what is that person doing to my family? And you wouldn't like that. So I don't understand why he would do that.

Did you notice the depth of these questions?

- What was so special about the shoes?
- Why did he want them so much?
- Did he feel the pressure to have what other kids had?
- What was his family like and where were they? Why was he out at night?
- Why would anyone try to steal somebody else's purse?

Did you note her own principles she expressed?

- You shouldn't do something to someone else that you wouldn't want done to you.
- You have to think about how others would feel.

Again, she has raised good questions and offered tentative answers. As teachers, we would want her to wonder why someone might want those shoes, and we appreciate her speculation that perhaps it had something to do with status in the group Roger was, or wanted to be, part of. She is tentatively drawing inferences about the motivations of the characters in the story. And Darian responds to her, suggesting a possible answer to her question, "Why would he want those shoes?"

> Maybe he wanted them shoes because he never had some. Maybe he never had a pair of new shoes. Maybe when he had a family, he always had his brother's old shoes. Maybe he wanted some new shoes.

While some of you reading this transcript might decide that Darian is telling us something about his own life, that perhaps he's never had his own pair of new shoes, we are unwilling to infer that. We, sadly, did not know him well enough to know if he was sharing a bit of himself. Perhaps his friends in the group did. What we did recognize is that Darian, while only in eighth grade, was showing compassion for someone else. He was able to think about this situation from Roger's point of view. If Darian can do this as a young teen, a time known for egocentric behavior, then we will be excited to see the young man he becomes. Darian is a compassionate reader.

We also noticed that there isn't any reluctance to try answering the question even though he knows that his answer, introduced with "maybe," might be wrong. He is willing to speculate. Perhaps there is some other explanation for Roger's desire for the new shoes—the uncertainty does not deter the student, he is not afraid of making a mistake, and he is not looking to the teacher for approval of his answer. He is simply participating, as any adult might, in an exploration of possible interpretations of the text.

The conversation continues with the next student extending Darian's speculation about his reasons for wanting a new pair of shoes. Darian had wondered if perhaps he had always worn hand-me-down shoes, and Lauren confirms that that's a possibility but speculates further that maybe it has something to do with Roger's peer group. Perhaps the shoes will give him status and make him feel popular. She mentions, apparently admiringly, that Mrs. Jones was "real considerate" with him.

> Oh, maybe something handed down or he just wants something to make him feel like popular for like one day at least. She still gave him the money. I think she was real considerate about him.

Then Shania speaks up, still concerned with Roger's situation, and she adds more questions:

> But you have to think about it. Do he have a family? Do he have a brother? Do—does he have a mom? Does he live with his mom or dad?

After the brief digression into biology, in which Darian reminds us he had to have a mother and a father, the next student wonders why Mrs. Jones took him in. She compares her own more cautious approach to strangers on the street with that of Mrs. Jones and wonders why Mrs. Jones is willing to risk taking him into her house:

> that doesn't mean I'm going to go run over and take him in my house. I wonder what was so good about him that she took him in?

Lauren's continued questioning about why she took Roger in shows us where her interests are. What made *him* so special? Then we have a brief remark about her efforts to neaten him up ("She cares so much about his appearance") after which the conversation turns to Mrs. Jones's situation, and to Shania's speculation that attempts to answer the question about why she might have taken him in:

> Maybe she had a son, but something happened
> to her son. And she just feel like, you know, she just
> took him in, at that point of time and just try to like
> show him right from wrong. Just from there. And maybe
> to teach him like he shouldn't be, shouldn't be trying
> to take people's stuff like that. It's still in his wrong.

Perhaps, as Shania offers, she had lost her son and now wants to treat Roger as if he were her own, taking a brief moment to care for him and to show him the difference between right and wrong.

After exploring that thought for a moment or two, Marcus, who has been quiet up until this point, introduces another idea:

> I think that she gave him the 10 dollars because when she was
> little, she tried to snatch people's pocketbooks, too.

He suggests that the gift of 10 dollars was motivated by a desire to atone for having stolen people's pocketbooks, too, when she was younger. He may have overreached slightly here, because there is no evidence that she has actually stolen in the past, but it introduces the possibility that her generosity comes, in part, from a feeling of guilt or shame for past offenses. In fact, Mrs. Jones at one point says, "I have done things, too, that I wouldn't tell God if he didn't already know." She may not have stolen pocketbooks, but Marcus is obviously right—she has done something in the past that she is ashamed of. Though this is the only comment Marcus offers, it's an important one and the other students respond respectfully by engaging with his idea.

And in the last paragraph or so of the transcript (the discussion continued on after we stopped recording), Tanisha affirms that Mrs. Jones did do something wrong and begins to explain that she would, like Mrs. Jones, say nothing about her own sins if she were trying to teach someone a lesson.

What We Learned

We've spent several pages working through a very short exchange in the classroom to try to show that a great deal can happen when we step to the side and allow students to assume some responsibility for control and direction of their thinking, allow them to influence the flow of talk, and restrain ourselves from controlling them too tightly. These students, we think, exhibited all of the following understandings and behaviors in this four-minute discussion:

- They worked on their own, without teacher direction.

- They noticed elements in the text—situations and behaviors of the characters, for instance.

- They recognized and allowed themselves to be surprised by what happened.

- They confirmed and even extended what their classmates had said.

- They brought the text to bear upon their world, and their own knowledge of the world to bear upon the text.

- They questioned and examined the motivations of the characters in the story.

- They grew aware of the social pressures upon the characters (the peer group pressure that may have driven Roger to need the blue suede shoes).

- They speculated about what they might do in the situations presented in the text.

- They asked many of the same questions that we, as teachers, would have included in our lesson plans.

- They asked a great many questions, and almost none of the questions were simple. They all required more than one-word answers.

- They began to think about ethical issues—the principle of behaving well toward others.

- They explored the text responsibly, seeking or offering evidence for their inferences.

To us, all of these behaviors suggest empowerment and responsibility. The students worked independently, paying close attention to the text, acknowledging and expressing their own values and principles, and listening to one another so that their understanding of the text could be built collaboratively. Did they change their minds about something? We aren't sure. They didn't state that explicitly, but that might have happened.

> **Some readings and conversations will give us sovereignty over own thoughts. Our independence emerges as our independent thoughts take shape.**

But let's say it did not. Not every text will change our minds about something. Perhaps most won't. Some texts will just entertain us. Some will confirm what we have thought, giving us more information that supports our point of view or simply affirming that our values have merit. And some will enable us to think differently. Some readings and conversations will give us sovereignty over our thoughts. Our independence emerges as our independent thoughts take shape.

Perhaps we saw in one or two of the comments the possibility of such change. If, for instance, later discussion focused on the possible significance of Roger's social group in leading him to value the blue suede shoes so highly that he would steal to get them, then we might have seen a slight change in the thinking of some of the readers about the appropriate balance between independent thinking by the individual and the influence exercised by the group. But we were impressed by the independence, self-reliance, and responsibility these kids demonstrated in their conversation.

And Now for a
Shorter Conversation

This is a conversation—much shorter—between two second graders who have just finished reading a very short nonfiction piece about matter. They were asked to talk about this short article by describing what surprised them. They chose to discuss the first two lines.

Student 1: I was surprised it said that matter is everywhere.

Student 2: Yeah. So, is it like air?

Student 1: Here, it says, "Matter is everywhere. Matter makes up everything."

Student 2: What does that mean? So air is matter. I thought air was air. Like this pencil is wood. Is it saying wood is matter?

Student 1: And my shoes are, hey what are my shoes made of? [Now sitting on the floor, the boys began a thorough examination of their shoes.] I think they are like some sort of cloth.

Student 2: So cloth is matter?

Student 1: Yeah. Matter is everything. So everything is matter.

Student 2: Hey, I guess that's what matters! Get it? That's what matters! [Now both boys give up reading and start telling everyone as they crawl around the floor, "Listen, that's what matters!" We left while the teacher was glaring at us for asking second graders, while sitting on the floor late in the afternoon, to discuss what had surprised them.]

While this conversation lacks the depth of the eighth graders'
conversation, they are tackling a tough topic, whether they thought
it *mattered* or not. Read it again and look for what shows you they are
well on their way to becoming empowered, independent readers.

Template for Conversation Note-Taking

When we have the opportunity to listen to a small-group discussion,
we find that keeping notes on a form, such as what's shown below,
helps us keep up with conversations. Do we use this all the time? No.
Do we use it when we want to assess how conversations are changing
throughout the year? Yes. Sometimes we are sitting with a group and
making fast notes as they are talking. Other times we have audio- or
video-recorded the group.

The ability to record discussions on a videoconferencing platform
allows you to return to conversations and analyze them. What you
want to move from is "That was a really good conversation" and
toward "Here's what happened that showed me my students are
becoming empowered learners."

Students	Questions to clarify confusions	Questions to clarify understanding	Responses to support others	Responses to extend or clarify others	Inferences, speculations, generalizations, conclusions

This form works for us, but you should make the one that works best for you.

13

The Second Most Important Way to Improve Comprehension

IF YOU'RE FLIPPING THROUGH THIS BOOK LOOKING for the chapter called "The First Most Important Way to Improve Comprehension," stop looking. We didn't include it. That's because the best way is simple and you already know it. You don't need to buy anything.

First, the First Way

The single best way to improve reading comprehension is to reread something. You do it all the time, perhaps without realizing it. You aren't sure about something or need to rethink it, so you reread.

That's why we are confused when teachers don't encourage students to reread books. Why not? We all enjoy listening to our favorite songs over and over again and often, during the umpteenth time of listening, we discover something about the song we had not understood during all the previous times. We enjoy the same great meal; in fact, some events are based on always serving the same thing. There are some holidays you probably celebrate that wouldn't be the same without the same traditions. We even know at least one rabid football fan who always wears the same jersey when his team is playing. "It's good luck for my team," the brother of one of us always explains. (His team only wins about half their games, so we think he needs a new jersey or they need a new fan.)

Some teachers might say some books aren't worth rereading, but that's the reader's decision, not the teacher's. And some teachers might say there are too many great books to share with students, so they can't let students take time to reread a book. You most certainly can if you believe in choice. And if you are "teaching" a book, stop worrying if a student read it the year before. These are kids who can't remember to bring their pencils to class most of the time. So what if they had read *Hatchet* in fourth grade? Yes, when they begin it again in fifth grade, they'll remember that at the end of the book, Brian is rescued. But as a fourth grader, they might not have noticed that about halfway through the book, Brian has a huge aha moment and as a result, everything about the tone of the book shifts, including the sentence length. Maybe they will see that now, as fifth graders. And maybe not.

If a student reads *New Kid* by Jerry Craft in sixth grade and now you want to share it with students through a book study in seventh grade, someone will probably say, "I don't want to read that book again." We've found this usually has little to do with liking or not liking a book. Some people don't like to reread a book. In that case, let them read a different book. We'd also encourage you to consider that it might be that they don't want to make another diorama, look up more vocabulary words, or draw another picture of the cover— if any of those were required with the first reading. Sometimes what they don't want to do again are the very same things we *never* do as a reader. Seriously, where do you put all those dioramas you make?

If a student wants to reread *Monster* by Walter Dean Myers repeatedly, we promise that each reading is allowing that student to figure out something new. And if another keeps returning to the picture books *Hair Love* by Matthew A. Cherry or *Your Name Is a Song* by Jamilah Thompkins-Bigelow, then there's a reason. That reason might remain unarticulated, but there's a reason. With each successive rereading, more is understood. So, the best and easiest way to deepen the understanding of a text is to reread it.

Finally, if you are worried what to ask about a book that students are reading for a second or third time, then we wonder if you are spending too much time focused on developing questions to help guide their thinking. Step back some and let their questions guide their thinking. Tell them you are excited they are returning to this book, and ask them to tell you what they noticed this time that they didn't notice the first time. Ask them what they took to heart the first time and how that differs from this time. And then let them reread. They'll learn something new about the book, and if they're lucky, about themselves. We promise.

And Now the Second Way

It's the *second* best way to improve comprehension that requires more discussion. And that's good that it requires discussion, because it has little to do with reading. It's all about talk.

Discussions That Aren't Discussions

If our students are to become independent, they must also become responsible. Somehow, we must convince them to assume a critical stance so that they are not manipulated by others. When we have them seated in front of us, we can suggest, even assign, texts that present various, perhaps competing, views. But they won't always be sitting in front of us. We have to somehow instill in them the habit of seeking out other points of view if they are to continue to do that when they are out of our classrooms. And one of the best ways to do that is through talk, genuine classroom talk.

Talk is hard to handle even within the four walls of the classroom under the best of circumstances, especially when controversial issues arise. Although a presentation or a demonstration, or—in college courses—a lecture, requires attention and perhaps some participation from the audience, a discussion absolutely demands it.

There are times when what passes for classroom discussion is only a simulation of discussion. When the teacher asks a question, waits for the students to respond, judges the responses so that she can dismiss the inadequate ones and approve of the better ones, and then moves on to the next question, what may look like a discussion is really an interrogation. Rather than a dialogue, it is a monologue in two voices. The teacher asks the question, to which she knows the correct answer, the student offers it (or doesn't), and then the teacher moves on. Essentially, she is providing a sentence with a blank, and the student fills in the blank. The point of view the students might have, the relevant experiences they may have had, the perceptions they might offer, and the possible questions they might ask, all are ignored. The text is all that matters. Usually, the questions that guide these discussions are monologic questions: they are questions to which teachers already know the answer. That's why this type of discussion rarely feels like a discussion. The goal is not to create understanding; it's to prove understanding. Or perhaps to prove that they did their homework.

Using the Three Big Questions for Conversation

If, however, talk begins with the students' responses to the text, we may be able to hold their interest and explore both the issues they want to consider and the issues we want to explore. For that reason, the first questions in the discussion of a text should focus on the effect of the text on the reader. We turn to what we call, and have written about in other texts, the Three Big Questions.

We call these the
Three Big Questions
and encourage
students to keep them
in mind as they read.

WHAT SURPRISED YOU?

The first of those questions asks, "What surprised you?" This
question focuses the reader's attention not simply on the text, but
on the impact of the text upon the reader. The follow-up question
may not even be necessary, because the students may feel compelled
to expand upon their answers to that simple three-word question,
but if it is needed, it is obviously, "Why?" The conversation will then
be about what aspect, or passage, or idea, or word in the text caused
the surprise and about the reader's own attitudes or thoughts that
caused him to be surprised. In other words, the talk will be about
both the text and the readers themselves. And young readers are
always interested in themselves.

As are older readers.

WHAT DID THE AUTHOR THINK YOU KNEW?

The second of the Three Big Questions is "What did the author
think you knew?" This question, too, asks the student to look at
the impact of the text. In particular, it asks where the student was
confused or felt the need for more information. Once again, the
ensuing conversation should focus upon the transaction the reader

has had with the text and invites attention to both the page and the person reading the page. Even though this question appears in the second position on the anchor chart, this is not a prescription that it must be asked second. Some students begin a conversation immediately with, "The author thinks I know what this word means, and I don't." That's fine.

WHAT CONFIRMED, CHALLENGED, OR CHANGED YOUR THINKING?

The last of the Three Big Questions, "What confirmed, challenged, or changed your thinking?" asks students to look back, probably after they have finished reading the text, maybe after both reading and discussing it, and reflect on how the experience might have changed their perceptions or their understandings of self, others, the text, and the issues addressed. We think this question is particularly helpful at the end of a unit. For instance, we observed a third-grade class over several weeks. At the beginning of their unit on the importance of honeybees, several students adamantly proclaimed, "I hate them! They sting." By the end, though, they had learned enough to alter their thinking. One reported, "I still don't like them because they do sting, but we have to have them. But I guess I don't hate them."

We want to move children from opinion to evidence, from reaction to reason. Teaching them to wonder as they are reading, "Hmm. What's changing my mind or challenging my thinking?," shows them that being open to change is good.

Students are usually passionate about themselves and their own thoughts, and so the difficulty should not be in sustaining the talk, but in ensuring that it is reasoned. Most students have been taught to value being right over thinking with an open mind, and so they may be inclined to cling to ideas even after reading and conversation have shown their ideas to be inadequate. But if the emphasis can continually be on the willingness to think and to change, we may be able to get them to value more than simple correctness in answering simple questions.

Talking to Discover

In the spring of 2020, we visited a school in New Jersey. It was our last school visit before everything shut down due to the pandemic.[18] These sixth-grade students had been reading with the Notice and Note Signposts and the Three Big Questions in mind for a couple of years, so they were well versed in them. We listened in on some small-group discussions they were having about *A Long Walk to Water*. You met Aliya in a previous chapter. Here's a look at a conversation from her book club group. We pulled up chairs (we have got to get bigger chairs for classrooms!) and asked what was surprising them the most as they read. Here's what we captured from one small group:

Student 1: At first, I was surprised that this was not like a really, really long time ago. I mean, part of it was. Part of it was in 1985. That was, I don't know, like a hundred years ago. The part that was in 2008, well, I was born in 2009, so that's not old. But they don't even have water. I didn't know that. I mean I thought everyone had, you know, *water*. Do you think that's still true? And is it just there, or are there places here?

Student 2: Where's that place? It's here. It was on TV where the water is bad? Like something is in the water?

Student 1: Oh, yeah. I think my brother did a report on it. It's somewhere. But I think they have water, just something got in it. Maybe that's just as bad, because maybe they can't drink it.

Student 2: Yeah. I was surprised that he walked across the desert barefoot. That really surprised me, like is that even

---

[18] A personal note about this visit: Thank you to Elizabethtown, NJ, for providing us with such a wonderful couple of days. Your students were kind, open, excited to see us, and so willing to share their thinking. And their thinking was insightful and delightful. We did not know when we left on March 12 that this trip would prove to be our last in-person visit to a school for a long time. But we could not have chosen a better last school to visit. We hope by the time you are reading this, we have been able to return for a face-to-face thank you.

real? Can you do that? The other thing that surprised me was all the Again and Again about water. Nya is always talking about having to go to the pond to get water, and then Salva is always about looking for water. I got it. There's not enough water.

Student 3: There's also all these Tough Questions. Like when Salva and them, they came across the people in the desert who were dying of thirst. You know, *really* dying of thirst. And he didn't know if he should give them water. So, yeah, you had the water again, but I thought the Tough Question was more important. Does he give away his water to help someone or save what he needs?

Student 2: Right. I'd like to think I'd share, because, you know your parents are always saying to share, but I've never had to wonder about sharing if it was about staying alive. Now that I think about it, they just want me to share easy stuff, like my toys or something.

Student 3: I know. I think that's why, it's like this book, well, it's both easy and hard. You know? The words are easy and I like it that the chapters are short. So, it's like, easy. But it's not. I love this book because in some ways it's the hardest book I've read without having to be hard. I don't know how to explain it. I mean it's about hard things, and it's really making me think. [pause] I looked it up. It's true. This book. So, this really happened. I don't think I could have survived like he did. I mean if I lost my family and didn't have anything. I don't think I could do this.

Student 2: Maybe you could if you had to. I mean, maybe he didn't think he could either. Remember how his uncle just kept saying to walk to that tree or that rock? That's how he kept him going. Maybe that's what you have to do. Like just do a little. And then you do a little more. I bet you could do it, too, like Salva.

Student 1: Do you think his name really is Salva? That sounds like salvation.

Student 2: Oh, that's cool. I hadn't even noticed that.

Student 3: Or, spit. No, not spit, but you know, um, saliva. Like that's water. Maybe when you read his name you're supposed to think of water. [Pause.]

Student 1: That's gross. [Giggling begins.] No one would name their kid Saliva. [Laughter emerges.] Or Spit.

We left this group before they decided to do something with their newest revelation. . . .

Unpacking Their Talk

This is an important conversation to consider, even though it began with some deep thoughts about what we humans can accomplish when we must and ended with a discussion of spit. If you have taught any grade for more than about a week, you understand this ability to move from the insightful to the ridiculous in one sentence.

But as we listened to their conversation, we realized there were many things students did not discuss. They didn't discuss the side-by-side stories of Nya and Salva. They didn't discuss why there was a war in Sudan. They did not ask where Sudan was. They didn't want to know if the war was still ongoing. They have so much to still discover.

Simultaneously, we noticed all they did discuss. They were astounded that parts of the world still struggle to have clean drinking water. They remembered that Flint, Michigan, has water that is not potable. And they recognized something we wish more of us would remember: the most important lessons in life don't have to come from texts with the highest Lexile levels. Because this book doesn't require a lot of heavy lifting with syntax and vocabulary, students were able to grapple with the important issues: Would they help someone in need if it meant harming themselves? How would they muster—

if they could—the fortitude to keep going despite overwhelming obstacles. And how did they get to that discussion? We asked them "What surprised you?" And then we got out of the way.

Conversing, Not Debating

Keep reminding the students that their conversations are not debates and that their purpose should not be to defeat the other people with whom they talk but rather to learn from them. Collaboration, rather than combat, is what we are seeking. Encourage students to ask one another for clarification, for an example, for evidence, and for reasons. Encourage them always to be willing to change their minds as they hear a new perspective or a new argument. Value changing of minds, when appropriate, as an indication of intellectual maturity.

The problem, of course, is that at some point we have to loosen our hold over kids. We want them to be able to have rational conversations on their own, but as a quick glance at our politicians reveals, many people revert to combative, rather than collaborative, conversations. Many politicians depend upon affiliation rather than reason. They value loyalty over logic. How, then, is the teacher to encourage independent discussion of texts? In the classroom he can raise questions, perhaps put students in groups, offer his own silence for a time and expect, perhaps require, the students to fill that silence with their own thoughts. He can manage, direct, encourage, and even force something that looks much like conversation, but when those students go out on their own will they be able to discuss productively the texts they encounter?

They have, after all, almost no models of good conversation to draw upon. There are exceptions,[19] but most television shows in

---

[19] Steve Allen's *Meeting of Minds* aired on TV from 1977 to 1981. Here, famous historical figures came together to discuss significant issues as the actors who portrayed them responded as their figures would have responded. Bill Moyers, an acclaimed journalist, also hosted a program in the 1970s, which he revived from 2007 to 2010 on PBS, titled *Bill Moyers Journal*. Now, podcasts "With Friends Like These" and "Pod Save the People," along with almost any of the ones listed on https://hiplatina.com/latinx-podcasts-listen/, offer examples of civil discourse during these uncivil times.

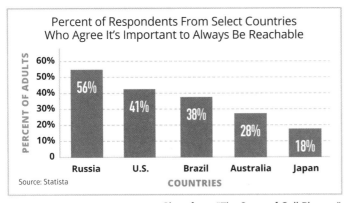

Chart from "The Story of Cell Phones"

which talk is featured consist of questions and answers, with the host as the interrogator and the guest as the interrogated. They are often adversarial and argumentative, with each person trying to win the argument, rather than being cooperative, with both parties trying to arrive at sharper understandings and clarified visions of the issues under discussion. They are more like debates than conversations, and the participants often seem more intent upon "winning" than upon sharpening their understanding.

Instead, you are looking to support a student's willingness to rethink positions. We've found that a reflection log, used sparingly, helps students listen carefully. Fourth graders had read an article found on the Scholastic site titled "The Story of Cell Phones." Part of the article included a chart (shown above). After reading the article, students wrote some reflections (shown below), talked with a partner, and then returned to their reflection log.

This change in thinking—a clarification followed by a new question—is to be applauded. The student doesn't realize that she

What did the text say?	What do I think about this?	What did my reading partner(s) say?	What do I think now?
About 55% of people in Russia say imp to have a cell phone. Only 40% in U.S.	This surprised me. Everyone I know has a phone or will get one when they are older.	Leila said it didn't say they had a cell phone, just said they thought it was important to be reachable. She says that is different.	I hadn't thought of that. I was thinking it was the same. Maybe more people than 40% have them here just because they want them. Not sure what this means about being reachable.

Student Reflection Log

got something wrong, but instead realizes her friend interpreted this information in a way that led her to rethink the chart. Rethinking is always to be lauded.

Using the Notice and Note Signposts to Empower Readers

And it's in that rethinking that we begin to reconsider the vision we hold of ourselves and others around us. As we thought about the process of becoming empowered through reading, we took a closer look at the Notice and Note Signposts. (Again, if this is a new term to you, you might pause here and take a look at pages 196–201 in the Appendix.) What we realized is that while the Notice and Note Signposts help students read for deeper understanding of the text, they also lead to deeper understanding of themselves—if you add what we call Empowerment Questions. Take a moment to look at the two charts on the next two pages.

We want to help students think about how a text might have changed them by giving them another question to consider after they've discussed the anchor question. We tell students to turn to this final column when they think it's appropriate. Our goal is for students to reflect on what the character or person has learned/experienced and then contemplate what they will take to heart. The questions in the final column provide a scaffold as students learn to read with such a mindset. We want them able to move from reporting that this book was "good" to thinking how it was good for them.

Those questions in the final column, the empowerment questions, aid students as they move from thinking about the text to thinking about the impact the text has upon their lives. The Notice and Note Signposts have helped thousands of children and teens think more about a text; now, let's let them help kids think about how a text can help them forge themselves into someone they perhaps never expected they could be, and help them forge a world they had only imagined.

Fiction Signposts

Signpost in Book	Definition of Signpost	Anchor Question for Signpost	Empowerment Question
Contrast and Contradiction	A character behaves or thinks in a way we weren't expecting	Why is the character acting or thinking this way?	When have changes in the way I think or act shown I'm changing?
Aha Moments	A character's realization of something	How might this change what the character does next?	What aha moments am I having about myself?
Tough Questions	Questions characters raise that reveal what they are worried about	What does this question show about the character?	What tough questions am I feeling as I read this book?
Words of the Wiser	Advise or insight offered to the main character	What's the life lesson and how will it affect the character?	What's the life lesson and how might it affect me?
Again and Again	Events, images, or words that occur again and again	Why does this author keep bringing this up again and again?	Does anything in this book remind me of something that happens again and again in my life?
Memory Moment	A recollection by a character that is brief but important	Why was it important for the character to share the memory?	What memories of my own does this book call to mind?

Nonfiction Signposts

Signpost in Book	Definition of Signpost	Anchor Question for Signpost	Empowerment Question
Contrast and Contradiction	A sharp contrast between what we would expect and what is happening	What's the difference and why does it matter?	How are these people's actions or thoughts different from my own?
Extreme or Absolute Language	Language that leaves no doubt about a situation or seems to exaggerate or overstate a situation	Why did the author use this language?	What does this language make me think about or how does it make me feel?
Numbers and Stats	Specific quantities or comparisons to depict the amount, size, or scale	Why did the author use these numbers or amounts?	Do these numbers raise any doubts? Do they affirm what I was thinking?
Quoted Words	Comments of someone who is an expert on the subject or someone who witnesses an event	Why was this person quoted or cited, and what did it add?	Did this quote raise any questions for me?
Word Gaps	Vocabulary unfamiliar to the reader	Have I seen this word? Does the context help? Does it look like a technical word?	What do I want to do now that I've recognized I don't know this word?

These Empowerment Questions lead us toward our ultimate goal: creating independent readers.

PART III
Hope

Books are keys that unlock the wisdom
of yesterday and open the door to tomorrow.

—Supreme Court Associate Justice
Sonia Sotomayor

We chose this art by Lulu Delacre, who illustrated *Turning Pages: My Life Story*
by Sonia Sotomayor, because it so beautifully represents the journey into the
future that books offer us.

14

The Independent Reader

BUT NONE OF THE TALK MATTERS IF OUR STUDENTS aren't reading. And when the talk turns to independent reading, it's easy to connect that to a level of books students can read on their own. But that's an easy definition. If you can't decode the word *Ganoob* the way someone has decided it should be decoded, then you can't read the book at an independent reading level. We want to ask you to reconsider the term *independent reading*, reenvision what it could mean in a classroom and, more importantly, in students' lives.

It's gone by several names. It's been called "The Revolutionary War," "The American Revolution," and "The War for Independence." The British apparently call it "The American War of Independence." We have also heard it referred to as "The American Insurrection,"

but that was in a pub and the term was uttered by a hostile gentleman who was in no way representative of the British educational system or a spokesman for the British people. And perhaps he had imbibed one pint too many.

The first four names use the words *independence* and *revolution* (or the derivation, *revolutionary*) twice. The term *insurrection* complicates the issue, so we'll simply disregard it here—irresponsible, perhaps, but convenient. The first two terms, however—*independence* and *revolution*—suggested some interesting comparisons with the notion of "Independent Reading," which is the subject of this chapter, and in some ways, of this entire book. Not that we are suggesting that we need a war to achieve independence in reading, though many far too easily adopt the jargon "reading wars" and "phonics wars."

Freedom and Discipline

But the term *independence* does have a history. It suggests independence *from* something. In fact, the word *independent* is so often followed by the word *from* that the two almost seem to be one. *Independence* suggests freedom from some control or restraint or direction. *Independence* suggests "doing it on your own," free from guidance or help, or at least with less guidance and help than was previously needed.

The colonists came to the New World for a variety of reasons. One set of reasons can be summed up as economic. The British monarchy encouraged settlement of new colonies as a way to make more money for the monarchy, and so some came to set up businesses. Some came in search of gold for themselves, and some craved the adventure of setting forth to a new land. Other reasons were religious. Protestant groups wanted freedom from religious restrictions imposed by the king. And some came because they believed the New World offered them a better life, one distanced from poverty, disease, and war. Ironically, as they sought independence *from,* they simultaneously denied independence *to* First Nations people, enslaved Africans, and any person of color.

In time, achieving distance from the king was not enough. The colonists wanted personal freedom, freedom from taxation, and freedom from any governmental hold on them by the monarchy. Independence was conceived, debated, declared, fought for, and achieved. The Declaration of Independence was signed in 1776, and the decisive battle was fought at Yorktown in 1781. The war lasted about seven years—not that long in the span of history. The change from colony to country was revolutionary rather than evolutionary. Independence did not emerge slowly and gradually. Instead, it was seized. The Revolutionary War had freed the colonies from Britain.

When we carry the term *independent* into the world of reading, it may suggest both the idea of "revolution" and the notion of "freedom from." Both are appealing, and possibly dangerous. Consider the idea of "revolution."

Revolution or Evolution?

Independence in reading may not be achieved by revolution. It may be more evolutionary than revolutionary. It may take more time to move our students to independence but, luckily, we have 12 years rather than the mere seven the colonists required. Nonetheless, sometimes we leap quickly and may not move our young readers toward independent reading as gradually and patiently as perhaps we should. In some cases, independence has been abruptly imposed:

> "We are going to start independent reading in this class. Go to the library, pick a book, and we'll each spend 10 minutes a day reading it. Complete this log and be ready to discuss it when you finish."

Independence in this scenario has some similarities with the word as it is used in "The War for Independence." It is abrupt and violent. Students have been moved suddenly from dependent reading—

reading controlled, assigned, mediated, and assessed by the teacher—
to independent reading—reading selected, sustained, and evaluated
by the students themselves. In this scenario, transition from
dependent reader to independent reader happens,
or is supposed to happen, overnight; the transition
from dependent colony to independent nation
happened, if not overnight, over a short period of
time in a spasm of violent activity. The similarity is
in the abruptness, the suddenness, of the change.
A revolution, rather than an evolution. Our
students may respond better if we take a somewhat
more patient approach.

> **"Independence in reading may not be achieved by revolution. It may be more evolutionary than revolutionary."**

    There is a dramatic difference, too, between the independence
the colonies achieved in the Revolutionary War, and the
independence we hope our young readers will ultimately achieve.
That difference is, of course, that in the Revolutionary War, the
colonies were seizing independence from Britain; in the classroom
we've imagined, the students are having independence imposed
upon them. The students haven't rebelled to seize it; rather, they
have suddenly had independence thrust upon them. In the war, the
ruling power, Britain, did what it could to prevent the colonies from
achieving independence; in the classroom, the ruling power, the
teacher, will do whatever is possible to confer independence upon
the students, whether they want it or not.

    Some of the students won't want it. It is easier, as some students
have told us, to leave everything in the hands of the teacher. Let the
teacher select the book, assign how much is to be read each day, ask
the questions, evaluate the answers, manage any discussion that takes
place, lead them to the correct interpretation, decide what writing is
to be done, and announce when it is time to put that book back on
the shelf and take up a new one.

    But such instruction, even though students may be comfortable
with it, is likely to produce dependent rather than independent
readers, readers who need a teacher—or someone else—to think for
them. Unfortunately, there won't be a teacher around later, when

they might really need one. There won't be a teacher around to select and assign their reading of documents that will shape their lives and assess how well they have comprehended them: reports on climate change that might influence what they do or avoid doing, events in our country's history that have been deliberately overlooked in some schools and some texts,[20] debates among political candidates who might push their society in one direction or another, works of fiction or poetry that might shape their understanding of human possibilities and responsibilities.

Once they leave our classrooms, those students will have to deal with texts on their own, independently. They will have to decide which texts matter, selecting them themselves. They will have to give themselves their own assignments, finding in their own minds the motivation to read. And they will have to assess how well they have done that.

At least, we would hope that they would deal with those texts independently. They won't have to. There will be plenty of people around eager to tell them what to make of texts. There will be commentators, religious leaders, advertisers, politicians, all eager to tell them how to think and what to think. There are a great many people out there who hope that the readers who leave our schools will not be independent thinkers but will be malleable and manageable and compliant. Which brings us to the second point.

Freedom From...

The colonists achieved freedom from Britain. But it was not the giddy freedom of the kite whose string has broken and that flies merrily away on the breeze, untethered, uncontrolled, free from all bonds and restraints. Instead, the colonists, in freeing themselves from oppression, incurred obligation. They were free from British taxes;

---

[20] For instance, we have taught about the Boston Tea Party but not the Tulsa Massacre. We teach, in economics, about Wall Street, but not about Black Wall Street; we teach about Marie Curie but not about Carlos Saavedra Robles.

but they had to figure out their own taxation system. They were free from British law; but they had to write their own. They were, in sum, free from the British government; but needed to design their own. The independence they had achieved had made them not just "free *from*. . . ," but "free *to*. . . ."

And perhaps "free to. . ." might more accurately be phrased "obligated to. . . ."

So it is with independent reading. The independent reader may be free from many things. The teacher may not assign the text to be read independently, he may not prescribe when it is to be read, he may not require a paper about it, he may not quiz or test the reading. But that freedom comes with an obligation for the reader to assume responsibility.

With pleasure reading, the burden of responsibility is light.

The reader simply has to be aware of what he likes and what he doesn't like. Unless he simply picks up the skinniest or closest book, he'll need to know something about the choices available to him. He'll need to know the authors he likes, the genres he is happiest with, the social, political, and scientific issues he is concerned with. But most readers, given some opportunity to form their own tastes, should be expected to know what's needed to make those decisions.

The reading we do to pass the time doesn't seem to require a great deal of us, though it's probably a good idea to reflect on even our most casual reading. We might ask, for example, what values seem to be assumed and possibly promoted in the books we read for casual entertainment. Without such reflection, we might not notice that the writer seems to promote violence as a way of solving problems. Perhaps the writer implies that one race is inferior to another or shows a bias against certain religions. An independent and responsible reader would be alert to the possible influences upon his own thinking by such texts. The writer's biases may have a subtle influence even on the casual reader. Much of our reading, however, unless we are content with pablum, with doing little or no thinking, with, as Neil Postman (1985) put it, "amusing ourselves to death," will ask a bit more of us.

With other reading—less light, possibly—the independent reader, even free from tests on the contents of a text, is not free from the obligation to think responsibly. Given a text, for instance, about some aspect of the physical world—objective reality—the independent reader is responsible for considering evidence, logic, and authority. When reading a text that is based on evidence that is well and persuasively reasoned, that comes from a reputable authority, and that is confirmed by other texts, the independent reader is responsible for taking what he has read into account. To disregard it would be irresponsible and potentially dangerous. If the text demonstrates that certain facts are so, then to deny that, much as we might like to, would be simply ridiculous. It would be a betrayal both of the community and of the self.

> "When reading a text that is based on evidence that is well and persuasively reasoned, that comes from a reputable authority, and that is confirmed by other texts, the independent reader is responsible for taking what he has read into account. To disregard it would be irresponsible and potentially dangerous."

Much of our reading will be problematic. It will deal with complicated issues and conflicting values and will require us to consider not only what is but also what ought to be. The COVID-19 pandemic illustrated that for us. We can't very well dispute that the virus killed a lot of people, though we may argue about precise numbers or about the ways in which we obtain the information; but we can discuss the decisions we, as a society, make on the basis of those numbers. The information will have implications for the health of the citizenry, for the education of our children, and for the economy of the country, if not the world.

We are educating students to participate in that process.

The Criticality of the Independent Reader

The importance of an independent reader is suggested by Wolf in her comment about the beauty of the reading brain's capacity to understand "the written word as the basis for generating new, never-before-encountered or shared thought" (p. 135).

It is the vision of "new, never-before-encountered or shared thought," that is important. If it is the "new," the "never-before-encountered," that we are seeking, then we may not be able to lead students to it; we may instead have to free them to find it. Independent reading is not simply reading independently, free from the teacher's control and direction—it is *reading that leads to independence*, reading that may generate new and previously unimagined ideas about who we are, who we might become, how we might function in the world. It is that sort of reading that might solve the problems our students, as they have poignantly told us, want to address. It is that sort of reading that might answer the questions that matter to them.

And those questions are not the ones we have prepared for Friday's quiz. The quiz questions usually look to what we can extract from the text, not what we might create from it. In other words, they look to the past. Many of our students are not satisfied with the answers we have come up with. Ask Greta Thunberg if she is satisfied with the responses of adults to climate change. Independent reading should help our students find what we have been unable to find. What we are seeking is not so much *independent reading*, as it is *independent readers*—readers who will ask their own questions and generate their own answers.

And if those questions are about personal issues, not only will we be unable to find them for our students, but we probably have no right to find them for our students. Who are we to tell them how they must feel and what they must think? The students who read Patricia Polacco's *Bully*, for example, and decide that they have to stand up for the victims, regardless of the sacrifice, will have made a decision on their own. Certainly, we can't tell students that they must do this, that they have to suffer the consequences of taking courageous action. Those who decide that they can't endure the consequences of standing up for the victims and so will choose to remain silent have made a decision. And that silence will speak loudly. We may not be happy with it, but it is not our right to tell them how they must exercise their independence.

All we have the right and responsibility to ask of them is reason, evidence, and explanation. This means we must probe beyond the response, "I just like it." "I don't agree" is not enough. Why not? Based on what? Change is hard—as we've said repeatedly in this book—because to hold one set of beliefs in mind while reading facts that might contradict those beliefs requires effort—sustained effort. But to be an independent reader, one has the obligation to do the thinking demanded by that contradiction.

On personal matters, especially, students must do their own thinking. We, during our years with them, have the golden opportunity of sharing with them the power of reason, the support of evidence, and the need for cogent explanation. And we have the opportunity to show them that reading lets them see beyond themselves, beyond their own limited world, to the greater world with all its rich diversity. We can only show them that reading can open a world of possible if the books we set before them are books that let them read beyond themselves, beyond the person they see in the mirror. Yes, we want them to see themselves, but even more, we want them to see others.

What we are after is not so much independent reading in the sense of attaining a particular Lexile level or being given the permission to read from the orange bin. It's not a time during class when choice is finally allowed. We are looking instead for the independent reader, one who is a responsive and responsible reader, one informed by reason and directed by purpose. One who reads with an open mind, a willingness to change, and delight at discovering those yet-discovered thoughts.

15

Questions About Independent Reading

WE ARE ASKED A LOT OF QUESTIONS ABOUT
independent reading. We thought we'd spend some time answering
some of those questions.

1 **What exactly is independent reading?**
We started thinking about our answer by asking teachers to
share their definition of independent reading. We ended our
research by reading Plato (c. 428–348 BCE), Cicero (106–43 BCE),
and Augustine (354–430 CE). No, we didn't get lost or sidetracked.
Reading—*our* independent reading—did what reading ought to do: it
raised more questions, so we had to keep reading. Why did Plato have
a negative opinion regarding silent reading even as he was writing his
dialogues? Why was Cicero a fan of silent reading? Why did Augustine

record amazement when he saw the Bishop of Milan reading silently? Why did each write about *lectio tacit*, silent reading?

Two texts, *A History of Silent Reading* (Fischer) and *Silent Reading in Antiquity* (Knox), taught us that silent reading—which meant reading independent of the orator—allowed for personal thoughts and that's why it was discouraged by most societies. The words inscribed on the clay tablet or scroll were a stand-in for the author. The reader was a reciter. No interpretation by reader or listener was wanted. Becoming a reciter was a slow and tedious task. So, apart from the most learned, who was taught to recite? Slaves. The aristocracy didn't waste their time on this task; they sent their slaves to learn that skill.

In 1439, Johannes Gutenberg (like Sequoyah, a forger of metals) invented the moveable-type printing press, giving more people access to more printed texts. People wanted to read their texts silently. Punctuation and spelling became standardized, so reading was easier. People enjoyed their independent thoughts, which urged on the Reformation and the Renaissance. Oral reading had a new cause: to keep the ignorant *ignorant*. Silent reading had a new cause, too: to allow independent thought. Now who could not learn to read? Slaves. Immigrants. Women. The poor.

While the term "silent reading" has been around since at least Plato's time, the use of the term "independent reading" is an early 20th century invention. It's a school term to describe a time during the day when students choose what they want to read. The term isn't used outside of school. When was the last time you left a party saying, "I must get home. I have some independent reading to do"?

Plato warned that silent reading would lead to interpretative thought, and Cicero thought "much greater pleasure can be experienced in reading them [poetry and songs] than in hearing them" (Knox, p. 427). Augustine was shocked to see the Bishop of Milan reading silently. Plato's, Cicero's, and Augustine's thoughts represent the reactions we see in schools today. Enter Plato as we hear, "Kids can't read independently. They might not understand the book correctly." Cicero echoes in our minds when we meet teachers and principals committed to independent reading knowing it brings pleasure and knowledge. And we think of Augustine when someone remarks that "just reading" is not valuable. We feel the same shock Augustine recorded feeling, though for a different reason.

2 How many books do I need for my independent reading program?

A lot.

No matter how many books you have, get more. Watch which ones kids like the most and get more of those or different titles by that same author, or more of that genre. Ask kids what books they like. Buy those.

3 Where do I get my books?

We have no idea.

We really think the question is, "Will someone else pay for my books in my classroom?" Our experience is, "No." Occasionally, if you're lucky, you'll be in a district that will hand you some money to buy some books. Or, you'll come across a grant (we list some grant opportunities in the Appendix on page 202). But too often, we find that teachers must pay for their own books.

That said, we disagree with this practice of expecting teachers to pay for their own classroom libraries. If science labs need lab equipment, if band halls need instruments, if history and geography classes need maps, if basketball teams need basketballs, and don't get us started on all that football teams need—if they need this equipment and receive it (though we've seen grossly under-equipped science labs), then why language arts classes are not brimming with books astounds us. So, we encourage you to be selective. Tell your department chair or principal, "Here are the 100 books I need this first semester and here are the 100 books I need next semester." Or 200.

If you do not yet have a classroom library, be careful about saying, "I need 1,000 books." Yes, you might want to build toward that, but from 50 books to 1,000 books can be daunting. You need storage; an arrangement system; an idea of how to know which students have which books; a plan for talking about books; a censorship policy in place in case a parent demands that a book be removed from your classroom library; and your own inventory system so you can make sure you are building an inclusive library. Build your library the same way you build anything else—starting with a strong, solid foundation.

And keep up with how much money the football team (or soccer team or baseball team or whatever sport is big in your area) receives. Did they get new equipment for $25,000? That equipment will serve a handful of kids. The books in the ELA classrooms will serve all kids. Be loud. Be pushy.

The underfunding of classroom libraries is one area where we see systemic racist policies at play. Schools in economically depressed neighborhoods often lack the necessary equipment for rigorous, robust, exciting, creative learning. Yet other schools, in the same district, in wealthier neighborhoods turn to PTOs and PTAs to raise the money needed for extra equipment—from 3D printers to black box theaters to high-magnitude microscopes to the newest weight equipment in the field house to classroom libraries. Parents in those schools often have bake sales that yield thousands of dollars, not because those baked cookies are better than the ones in other neighborhoods, but because those parents—many of them—can simply write big checks. And do. They didn't want to bake the cookies in the first place.

4 **How many minutes should they read a day?**
Again, a lot.

For a more complete answer, we must consider what constitutes reading during independent reading time and why the amount does matter.

First, independent reading time is not the same as grab-a-book-and-flip-through-the-pages time. We think that practice is better called, well, grab-a-book-and-flip-through-the-pages time. The only thing that is independent about that is that we let kids grab the book they want to grab.

If we're going to take important instructional time during the day for students to read a book, then we're going to suggest that prior to reading time, there needs to be an instructional lesson, one that can be practiced as they are reading. Much as the band director might remind the clarinets that before they play a long phrase, they need to take an extra-large breath, and then send them off to practice, teachers might remind students of something to consider before they send students off to read. For instance, you might want to remind students about one of the Notice and Note Signposts to keep in mind before they begin reading. We might say to third graders or ninth graders something like this:

> Before you begin your choice reading today, let's take just
> a moment to remind ourselves that characters will change
> as the plot progresses. It's important to notice those changes
> because that will help you understand characters and possibly
> the theme. Today, as you read, I want to you be aware of any
> Tough Questions you might notice. Remember, these are
> questions characters might ask themselves or someone else.
> They are those tough questions to answer that often show
> us what's worrying a character.
> When you notice those, ask yourself, "Why is this question
> important?" You can put a sticky note by any Tough Questions
> you notice, and we can talk about them later.

That's it. If you've never introduced Tough Questions before, then you might show some examples. In the picture book *Ira Sleeps Over*, Ira keeps asking if he should take his Teddy bear for his first sleepover. Seeing how he comes to his decision lets readers recognize a theme: always be true to yourself. In *Last Stop on Market Street*, CJ wonders why he and his grandmother must take the city bus. Watching him figure out the answer helps readers understand this book's theme: there is beauty all around us. In the novel for older students, *American Street*, the main character, who is navigating America without her mother who has been detained to be sent back to Haiti, wonders how she is supposed to navigate life without her mom. Teaching students to notice Tough Questions, helps them understand character development, and character development is important for the emergence of theme.[21]

Now, regarding how many minutes kids should read. We don't know. We don't know how long your classes are. We don't know what grade you are teaching. We can't suggest that kids read only 10 minutes day if you are an elementary teacher who sees kids in a reading block lasting 160 minutes. And if you are a secondary teacher, we can't say give students 30 minutes to read each period if you only see your students for 45 minutes each day.

We can say that the more kids read with support—and by support we mean the type of lesson we just shared—the more valuable the reading time will be. Flipping pages is not a valuable use of class time. We know that some of you reading this will disagree and would more happily support a time during the day when students read "just for fun" or "to enjoy the story." Our counter to that is that we do want them reading something they enjoy, that they choose, that is fun for them, BUT we think that the time reading is even more valuable if they are learning some habits of mind that improve or sharpen their thinking about what they are reading.

The chart on the next page shows what happens when we increase the amount of time kids spend reading by as little as 10 minutes a day. So, maybe our answer to what apparently was not an easy question is "however many minutes they are spending reading, have them read 10 minutes more."

---

[21] We are not suggesting that any one book has only one theme. These were examples of single themes that readers might come to recognize as they read with this Signpost in mind.

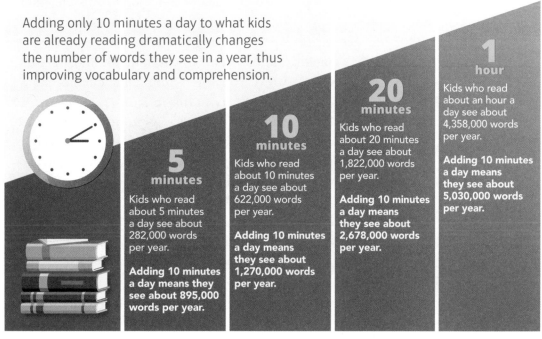

Adding only 10 minutes a day to what kids are already reading dramatically changes the number of words they see in a year, thus improving vocabulary and comprehension.

5 minutes
Kids who read about 5 minutes a day see about 282,000 words per year.

Adding 10 minutes a day means they see about 895,000 words per year.

10 minutes
Kids who read about 10 minutes a day see about 622,000 words per year.

Adding 10 minutes a day means they see about 1,270,000 words per year.

20 minutes
Kids who read about 20 minutes a day see about 1,822,000 words per year.

Adding 10 minutes a day means they see about 2,678,000 words per year.

1 hour
Kids who read about an hour a day see about 4,358,000 words per year.

Adding 10 minutes a day means they see about 5,030,000 words per year.

Adapted from Adams (2006) with baseline data from Anderson, Wilson, and Fielding (1988).

5 Do I need to give kids choice over what they read?

Yes.

Do you have to give them choice all the time? We don't think so. We know some will disagree and have significant reasons for their decision. We happen to think there are advantages for readers to occasionally read a book others are reading. A community sharing the book has a chance to ponder similar questions, has a chance to share moments of excitement or sadness in a book. We think kids and adults are hungry for community. We take as our evidence the millions of people who pick up an Oprah's Book Club selection. That might not be the most scientific of studies, but the *n* is huge. Other examples of adults enjoying book clubs are the hundreds of teachers who each summer join the Book Love Foundation summer reading club. On a smaller scale, countless neighborhood book clubs bring five or so people together to enjoy the same title (and often a glass of wine). The point: sometimes we enjoy reading what others are reading.

Our concern with everyone reading the same book in a classroom is that too many teachers think this means students should all read the book the same way. So, everyone plods along one chapter at a time. We went into greater detail about this in *Disrupting Thinking*; consequently, we'll just say there are many ways to share a book with a large group. We don't have to plod together.

As much as possible, though, give students choice. And if you think no choice is possible, then rethink the curriculum.

6 **What if students say they don't like to read?**
That's exactly what they will say, or at least some will say. Early in the year, start by reading aloud to students. While many students say they don't like to read, few say they don't like to hear a good story. Consequently, choose a good story and one that has a sequel or is by an author who has another book you can hand them.

If you have some students who love to read, even early in the year, let them begin the year by reading on their own. Gather a smaller group around you and share a book you know has always been successful with students. Is it best if they are following along as you read? Of course. But if you only have one copy of *The Boy at the Back of the Class*, then read that as they listen. If you have 10 kids listening and five copies, put them in pairs.

"Sometimes kids love to read what we don't count as reading material. Then they see themselves as nonreaders. In those cases, they don't have the problem; we do."

But don't give up. When students tell you, "But I hate to read," remind them that they might not like spinach, but that doesn't mean they don't like all vegetables, especially if we can expand our definition of vegetables to include macaroni and cheese! In other words, they might love graphic novels but have internalized that you don't see those as "real books." They might love comic books, but you don't allow those in your classroom. They might love gaming magazines but think you'll say, "that reading doesn't count."

Let's convince kids they are readers by respecting what they like to read.

You can move that video-gamer from that magazine to an interesting article on video games to a book about how online multiple-player games affect critical thinking, synthesis, multitasking, problem-solving, and collaboration in much the same way that parents long ago figured out how broccoli can be added to mac and cheese. Sometimes kids love to read what we don't count as reading material. Then they see themselves as nonreaders. In those cases, they don't have the problem; we do.

7 What if my principal says that kids shouldn't spend time "just reading"?

From Kylene: Early in my career, I was certainly one of those teachers who was seduced by the image of 30 seventh graders sitting quietly at their desks, or maybe at the front of the room in the several bean bag chairs (that I thought for exactly 15 minutes were a good idea to have in my classroom), deeply engrossed in some award-winning text.

The reality is that I had 30 seventh graders who would grab a book and fight for the four bean bag chairs so that the winner could take a ballpoint pen and poke holes through the vinyl so they could pull out the pellets and throw them across the room. Occasionally someone would actually turn a page of a book—but that book was usually the *Guinness Book of World Records*.

It took a while until I realized that a sustained silent reading time without some sort of instructional purpose wasn't improving comprehension (or at least usually not), and I'm not sure it was even improving joy of reading. Why not? Because I had not done the necessary planning. I didn't know enough about books those seventh graders might enjoy. I was choosing books for them I would enjoy. That meant I was excluding everyone who wasn't a 22-year-old, newly married, white, beginning-year teacher. So, my small library had too many females-as-main characters, far too many books with white characters, and far too many plots that focused on solving a single problem, usually over the course of a couple of days. I had not carefully considered my students. I did not see who they were. Oh, sure, I had administered a reading interest survey. It was, I say with much certainty, useless. Here's an example of one:

What types of books do you enjoy? _____ None _____

What was the name of the last book you read? ___ None ___

What are your interests? _____ None _____

Which do you prefer, fiction or nonfiction? _____ None _____

And so, with that information, I turned students loose in my small classroom library or the school library to find a book. Most just grabbed something, anything, to sit with it opened as they napped. Not all students. Teri Cummings was the most voracious reader I ever encountered, still to this day. Jody Ezernack was a close second. But they arrived that way. The best I can say is I didn't harm them.

We now avoid a lot of that fake reading by using what we call *directed independent reading* or *mediated independent reading*. That simply means that independent reading isn't something we do first for 10 minutes and then say we're done and move to the day's lesson. The reading students do is a part of the lesson. We talk with students about how authors show character development and then ask them to mark in their books—usually with sticky notes—places that provide examples of what we've just taught. For an example, see the answer to question 4 where we discussed reading with Tough Questions in mind.

When your principal says, "I don't want to see kids wasting time 'just reading,'" first, make sure he's right. Are they wasting time? Are you sitting at your desk trying to catch up on paperwork? Are kids on their cell phones texting each other? Have some fallen asleep? Are others just turning pages in a book? That's not a useful way to spend precious moments of class time.

A better way to make sure your independent reading time is best serving students is to teach a large-group or small-group lesson prior to the reading. Then tell them to keep those points you've just taught in mind as they read. As they read, circulate and quietly ask students to tell you what's happening. Maybe ask a few to quietly read aloud a passage they really enjoyed and tell you why. One of our favorite questions is always, "What's surprised you the most in what you've read so far?" Perhaps you turn to one of the Notice and Note Signposts and say, "Can you show me any Tough Questions you've noticed? What did those moments show you about the character?"

And remember, you know your students. When one looks back at the book, turns through pages, and says nothing, then something is going on with that student's interaction with that book. It might be so important to the student that he can't yet put what he's thinking into words. Or it might the wrong book and he's simply turning pages. You know your kids and know when it's time to say, "Let me circle back to you," or "Would you like me to help you find a different book?"

8 Won't some parents object to books that bother them?
Sure.

If parents object to their child reading a particular book, then we always respect that. If the student really wants to read that book, then we ask if the parents if they would be willing to read it along with the student so they can discuss it. If that's not acceptable, then we ask the student or the parents to find a different book. You will sometimes be surprised at what upsets parents. We will never forget the parents who were angry at us—enough to call the principal—for bringing in an article about the dangers of fracking. These parents in a town in Wyoming did not want their ninth graders to consider the possibility that fracking might be harmful to the environment. Another time, there was a parent of a fifth grader who objected to

Librarians have often gone out of their way to get books into the hands
of readers, as this photograph of a librarian delivering books shows.

our recommendation of *Because of Winn-Dixie* because there is an
absent mother.

What a parent can't do is tell you to remove a book so that other
children can't read it. If a parent does try to do that—or goes around
you to the principal—head straight to your librarian or principal and
make sure that the parents understand the process for challenging
a book. Make sure, now, that teachers in your school understand
the process. Don't be intimidated by the genteel smile of the kind
parent who is "only trying to protect all our children." She can
protect hers. Period.

Finally, also be sure to reach out to the National Council of
Teachers of English. This organization, over a hundred years old,
has been helping teachers handle censorship issues for a long time.[22]

Remember, you want kids to see themselves in some books and
see beyond themselves in others. This means you must be a reader,
a wide and inclusive reader. Seriously, if you don't like to read, then

---

[22] See Guidelines for Dealing with Censorship of Instructional Materials:
https://ncte.org/statement/censorshipofnonprint/

why are you teaching reading/language arts? Teach something else. Or do something else. Our nation is crying out for kids who will grow into adults who make careful, considered, responsible decisions for themselves and their communities. And that means reading. If you aren't a reader yourself, then how do you, to the best of your ability, help kids become what you are not?

And as you are building your classroom library (with funds you do not have and we were of little help in showing you how to find), remember to build an inclusive library. Look at your books and ask yourself whose voices, whose stories, whose histories, whose lives are represented in the books you have in your room, in your required reading list, in your assignments. Look carefully at the books shown in your room. How many books about First Nations people do you have? What's your ratio of books with white main characters to books with Black main characters? Are your books with Black main characters all books about sports or slavery? Do you have books with LGBTQ characters? Are your books that feature Latinx characters all about immigration? What religions are represented? What other countries are represented? Do you have books written and/or illustrated by BIPOC? If you teach younger students, do you have more books with characters who are animals than people? That's an easy way to avoid having people of color. Just let a mouse tell the story.

Ask yourself if you were not the person you are— for us that is white, cisgender, married, with grown children—but were Black or brown or gay or from a family with two moms or two dads or Muslim or biracial or deaf—would you be able to see yourself in your classroom library?

> **❝...it isn't choice if they don't have choice. Wide, encompassing, embracing, engaging, inclusive, joyful choice.❞**

If not, keep looking for ways to bring more books into your classroom. Some city libraries let teachers take large numbers of books out on loan for extended time. Check there. Some local businesses will partner with you to provide funds for books. Go in and ask. We are always surprised at the growing number of grant opportunities we find when we search "Grants for teachers to buy books." Take an afternoon and do a thorough search and then search again a month later. New grant opportunities appear often, especially in the spring and early summer.

9 Should children be told to read from certain levels during independent reading time?

No.

For teachers who choose to use leveled or decodable texts during their instructional day, that's about using leveled or decodable texts for some specific type of instruction. We'd rather see you use leveled texts than decodable texts, but we hear that the rat has returned to the mat while wearing a hat.[23] We also hear those are now called accountable texts. We think these contrived texts are rather ridiculous, but we're focused on independent reading here. In closing, during independent reading time, it isn't choice if they don't have choice. Wide, encompassing, embracing, engaging, inclusive, joyful choice.

10 My day is so full. Do I really need to make time for independent reading?

Yes.

The day you hear a football coach say, "Our day is really busy getting the field ready, learning plays, going through the drills. It's so busy that we just don't have time to actually let kids on the field to practice the game" is the day we'll say you don't need to make independent reading time part of your day.

In Texas and Florida, our states, that would be when hell freezes over.

---

[23] If you were not a teacher when the goal was to give young students texts with only decodable words (or nearly only), then, you missed the time when there were many short texts with gripping sentences, such as "The dog at the bog sat on a log." We understand some school districts are revisiting such instructional materials; thus, "The rat has returned to the mat while wearing a hat." Rhyming texts, such as *Hop on Pop* are much fun, but contrived texts with "the dog at the bog" leave readers in a fog.

16

From Transaction to Transformation

MOST TEACHERS WENT INTO EDUCATION TO "HELP kids," "work with kids," "encourage children to reach their potential," "share a passion" for whatever their passion is: science or math or literature or physical education or art or . . . . Maybe you, as that undergraduate in college or that first-year teacher, were not sure how you were going to do all that sharing, but you were excited to learn. You were excited to figure it out. You understood that, though you had much to share, you still had much to learn. Perhaps even without realizing it, you had acknowledged and embraced the importance of a dual role: teacher and learner.

You knew that to become the teacher you longed to be, you simultaneously had to be the learner you needed to be. You were willing to see yourself in two roles, roles so intertwined—interdependent actually—that you could not separate the teacher from the learner because you were both.

From Kylene: Consider this conversation I had with a student I'll call Shawn, who was taking my undergraduate English methods class at the University of Houston. The students had arrived for their 5 p.m. class after a full day of student-teaching. As always, they were excited to share what had happened that day. Shawn wanted to share first.

Shawn: Today was the best day. We were reading Ray Bradbury's "All Summer in a Day."[24] I had asked the question at the end of the story in the literature anthology that was "When did the students remember they had left their classmate locked in the closet?" I called on this student and he said, "Not until they came back in."

Okay. That was the right answer, but he didn't stop. This kid had more to say. He said, "How could they not remember that they had locked the one person who would have enjoyed the sunshine the most in a closet? How could they not remember that? That wasn't a joke. That was just mean. But did they know they were being mean? And if you don't really mean for it to be mean, is it still being mean? I wondered what I've done that has been that mean; you know I meant it to be a joke, but it wasn't to that person. To that person it was mean."

Kylene: And . . . [and we'll never know what I was going to say as Shawn had regained his steam after his pause for air].

---

[24] This short story tells of Margot, a nine-year-old who lived the first five years of her life on Earth. Now, living in underground tunnels on Venus, where the sun only shines for two hours every seven years, Margot is miserable and her classmates shun her, envious of her firsthand knowledge of Earth and sunshine. On the day when the sun will shine for two hours, in a moment of frustration and bullying, the classmates push Margot into a closet, lock the door, and forget about her. They rush out to enjoy the sunshine, finally understanding why Margot has been depressed. When the rain returns, they, with new appreciation for sunlight, march back underground and remember Margot. The story ends as they unlock the door and let her out.

Shawn: It was the first time, you know, that I put the textbook down and listened. I wasn't checking for a right answer. I was listening to his thinking. Like I could see him figuring out something important about *himself*. Then another kid started talking. She said that sometimes people say something about her and then they say, "Just kidding" or "Can't you take a joke?" She said that then she laughs, even though it still doesn't feel funny to her. Then another wondered when does a joke become mean? And another said you have to mean it to be mean before it *is* mean. But another said that when people say, "Just kidding" you can tell they really weren't. They just don't want to get in trouble.

Kylene: So . . . [And then Shawn concluded the lesson for me].

Shawn: I'm sorry. Not to interrupt you, Dr. Beers, but it was the best day yet. I barely did anything because they were all starting to have these, I don't know, like revelations on who they are or at least what they are doing and how their actions can hurt other people, and we didn't get through the questions and usually that would have made me worry, but this time, it was exciting. It was, *something*. I don't know. It made me feel so great to see them make their own discoveries.

Kylene: It's called good teaching, Shawn. You got out of the way so they could find their way.

Shawn: So, this was that transacting with text you had us reading about? That article . . . [he looked through his notes] "Mom, Wolfgang, and Me" by Dr. Probst?[25]

---

[25] Shawn was reading one of what I consider to be Bob's landmark articles. At this point in my career, Bob wasn't a friend or a writing partner. He was the person who had written articles and written *Response and Analysis*—a text that reshaped my understanding of the teaching of literature. Years later, Bob would visit my university classrooms and explain transactional theory himself. —*KB*

Now I can see it. They weren't just reading for what the story said, they were seeing more than what was in the story because they were living it, too. So, it meant more because it meant something to them. Right?

Kylene: [I nodded.[26]]

Shawn: Well, now I really don't know what to do because tomorrow they want to start doing something, like one suggested a "Just Kidding Hurts" campaign at school. That's not in the book.

Kylene: I see. [Shawn looked at me, waiting. *Now* he wanted me to say something, but *now* I didn't want to say a thing.] That's all I got, Shawn. What do *you* think needs to happen next?

Shawn: That's not helpful.

Kylene: Probably not. It's called getting out of the way.

Shawn figured it out and he let the kids go to work. Some put "Just Kidding Hurts" posters around the school, and every day for a while someone said something about being kind during the morning announcements. Someone else went on to write an editorial for the school newspaper. The history teacher asked Shawn what short story the kids had read because some of the students were connecting the story "All Summer in a Day" to the women's suffrage era they were discussing. Women, metaphorically, were locked away in a closet on a very important day, election day. They wanted to be able to vote. While we, as adults, might see the connection between that text and women's suffrage as a stretch, it was a meaningful stretch for the students and helped them think more about women's suffrage, which they were studying.

---

[26] But at this moment, to all of us, Bob was Dr. Probst, the guy who wrote the articles. He had written so much, for all I knew, he was dead. But, that's another story. —*KB*

Shawn wrote his final reflection for my class on Paulo Freire's *Pedagogy of the Oppressed*, a book I suggested he read. This landmark book, one we believe should be read by every teacher, helped Shawn understand why the "banking model of education" that Freire explains sees the teacher as the holder of knowledge and students as a piggy bank to be filled, should move, instead, to a model in which student and teacher are co-creators of knowledge. Freire explains that animals differ from humans in that animals are present-bound and cannot turn to their history, as humans can, to reenvision what their futures might be. Through dialogue, Freire explains, we allow others to construct their world or we oppress them by not letting them fully recognize their history. As Shawn considered all that Freire was writing, he wrote in a final paper:

> I go into a class as a white male. I have learned history that
> has been shaped by white males. And I have mostly read
> literature by white males. Like Margot who was locked
> away and denied what was rightfully hers, I fear
> I might do the same to my students. This is my last class.
> Now I'm supposed to be ready to be a teacher. I feel
> ready and don't feel ready. I think I will always be learning
> how to be a teacher. I think I will always be undoing
> a pedagogy of the oppressed.[27]

Yes, Shawn, all of us who are open to change, who are willing to think responsively and responsibly, all of us, to borrow from Freire, will always be in a state of becoming.

---

[27] Throughout his career—which continues as of the writing of this book—Shawn moved from being a teacher to a supervisor to an administrator. He now has his doctorate and is helping others learn that to be a teacher one must constantly be in the process of learning how to be a teacher. His time in my classroom was instrumental in my development of being a teacher and for all that he taught me, I remain grateful. —KB

Analyzing the Discourse

There is much to mine from Shawn's conversation with the class. While this is not a word-by-word transcription of his comments, it is recounted from detailed notes Kylene kept while doing her own study of how students (in this case, undergraduates) interact with texts and others. Let's look at just two of Shawn's statements.

"It was, *something*."

First, Shawn said, "It was, *something*. I don't know. It made me feel so great to see them make their own discoveries."

The word Shawn was searching for was *empowering*. It was empowering. Too often, we—teachers—are fearful of turning over power to students. And honestly, if you ask us if on a Friday afternoon if we want a room of empowered fourth graders, we're likely to say, "No!" But that's when we have confused "in power" with "empowered." Empowerment is not about letting go of the curriculum you need to cover, the classroom discipline you need so all can learn, the kindness and respect we want students to show for one another. Empowerment is about letting kids learn by asking, not merely by answering; learn by reflecting, not by receiving; learn by constructing, not by copying.

By letting go, Shawn wasn't diminished in his power. He didn't think he had to control the thinking or the discussion. He let go of urging kids to answer questions and instead let them discover their own questions. He felt energized because he stepped aside to let others put voice to their thoughts. He stopped suppressing that curiosity those eighth graders managed to bring into class with them. He said he saw them become more animated than ever. He discovered that if we could stop seeing teaching and learning as polarities but instead could recognize them as interdependent, then we, teachers, could stop defending our positions as those who know and who have the weighty job of imparting that knowledge.

He learned that teaching means giving students the freedom to discover. Not memorize. He saw firsthand how empowering it is to step to the side, watching as others realize that they have the ability to empower themselves, to become active learners and in those moments of learning to become their own teachers. Your role is not diminished when you give others the space and voice to empower themselves. Students look at you differently, not as an equal but as someone who sees *them*, sees their abilities and uniqueness, their curiosity and passion, their potential to discover their potential.

Students see that you recognize that as they learn more, more about themselves, about themselves in the world, about their interactions with others, about how they exist in this space and this time, they are *transacting*—to use Louise Rosenblatt's word (1938)— with the world. And in that transaction, they are helping to transform their reality.

Doing Something

"Well, now I really don't know what to do because tomorrow they want to start doing something, like start a 'Just Kidding Hurts' campaign at school. That's not in the book."

In that statement, Shawn had moved from Rosenblatt to Freire. Rosenblatt tells us that when we read, we certainly gather meaning from what's on the page, but that meaning is meaningless until it means something in our lives. That's the transaction. Freire (1968/1970) tells readers:

> In the problem-posing education, people develop their power to perceive critically the way they exist *in the world* with which *and* in which *they find themselves; they come to see the world not as static reality, but as a reality in process, in transformation* (p. 83).

Rosenblatt, in 1938, explained that meaning resides in the transaction between the reader, the text, and the world. Freire, in 1968, told us that once we stop seeing the world in which we live as static, then we have the opportunity to transform our reality.

And Harari, in 2018, stated "to change the world, you need to act" (p. 320).[28] And Shawn saw all of that play out in his classroom years ago.

Shawn's students wanted to *do* something. In that moment, they were moving from transacting with the text to transforming themselves, and perhaps in that transformation of themselves, they might also transform the world in which they lived. This need *to do* is too often reduced to doing an assignment, completing a project, finishing a review for a test. It is too rarely left undefined to see what "doing" means to students. In this case, though, the doing was authentic because it came out of the realizations the students had about themselves: "I wondered what I've done that has been that mean, you know I meant it to be a joke, but it wasn't to that person. To that person it was mean."

Shawn's students moved from reading the text to reading their lives to reading to change the world. They read to do. With this need to move to action, we should reconsider the BHH framework we presented in *Disrupting Thinking*. BHH stands for Book, Head, Heart. We think teachers have done a good job at helping students learn to notice what's in the book, to then think about what that information means to them, and to remember to ask students to think about what they take to heart. But perhaps there is a final step to BHH reading: "Now, what will you *do*?" So it becomes BHH-D reading.

[28] The authors of this book would like to express their gratitude to Rosenblatt, Freire, and Harari for publishing books in years that ended in the number eight. Without such cosmic delight, this paragraph might have been omitted.

Most of the time, students might choose to read another book by the same author or another book in the same genre or about the same topic. That's a great thing to do, and we wouldn't want you to create a mindset in which reading a book always means doing something. For us, that doing most often means pouring a glass of wine and finding someone to talk with about the book. That's it. But sometimes, what we read sends us out into the world to do something. We know that's true of students, too. These are some of the many comments teachers shared with us after their students finished reading something with the BHH framework in mind:

> *Wonder* helped me think about how I treat people. That was my heart lesson. Now I want to do something about the bullying in our school. [sixth grader]

> I just finished *The Hate U Give* and I took so much to heart. We're afraid of ICE because of one of our relatives, I can't say who, is here, you know, illegally. He's got to pretend to be invisible. This book, I mean it's about Black people, but it's about Black people being hurt because of racism, and I feel like ICE wanting to take back my relative to Mexico is because of racism, too. I want to do something to make this racism go away. [tenth grader]

> My heart thinking is you have to keep trying even when it is hard, like when she couldn't pound the rice and she felt sad but then her friend said he couldn't either the first time he tried. It made me think you always have to keep trying. I told my little sister that when she wanted to stop playing the piano because it was really hard. [second grader, reading *Jasmine Toguchi: Mochi Queen*]

> My head thinking was always wondering why Bud was so worried about rules. Then my heart thinking was that Bud didn't have anything else but his rules because he didn't really have a family. What I will keep in my heart is

that family is really important. And animals need a family, too. I am going to ask my mom if we can adopt a dog. Like, I really want a dog, but if she would read *Bud, Not Buddy*, too, maybe she would see that I want a dog to give him a family. [fourth grader]

While we had never anticipated the BHH framework as a tool for a child to get a dog, we were struck that this fourth grader, like all the others, found himself wanting to *do* something after he had read. Our second grader, in fact, had already moved into action as she encouraged her little sister to keep up with something—playing the piano—even when the pieces became more difficult.

The transactional nature of reading can lead to the transformational actions of the reader. For that reason, we want to build on our framework and encourage you to remind students that what they have taken to heart might inspire them to change: they might change their own actions, own words, own beliefs; or, they might be stirred to try to change the world around them.

To help, you might modify your BHH charts to something more like this:

17

Wondering and Wandering

MANY OF THE READING BEHAVIORS AND READING abilities we expect from students are based on norms—visions of what children should be able to do at specific points. In third grade, students should be able to read texts at this particular Lexile level. Why? This is surely one of those conceptual realities that has no basis in the physical world.

Some would respond, "That's because by college, kids must be able to handle texts written at this higher Lexile level." While we want students to be able to read the technical manuals they will be reading if they move to technical degrees or jobs, or the textbooks they will be reading if they head on to college, their ability will be determined more by their desire to read that text than the Lexile level. "Nope, Dr. Professor, this biology book is not at my Lexile level" just won't (or shouldn't) ever be uttered by a kid in Biology 101. More importantly, Dr. Professor won't be providing an anticipation guide or fill-in-the-blank questions for students to answer as they read.

Even more importantly, Dr. Professor won't care what the Lexile level of a text is. Dr. Professor probably doesn't know what a Lexile is, or give a damn.

Letting Them Just Read

The motivation to stick with a text when the text is tough must be developed in school. We worry that too often keeping kids reading "at their level" fails to teach them how to handle a text that stretches their thinking. Furthermore, this practice of marching students from one level to the next assumes that reading growth is linear and that it's the same line for all students.

There is nothing normative about reading, and there is no single template that would describe the highly skilled reader at a young age, the reluctant reader who has not yet found the book she wants, or the striving reader who has not yet moved past some foundational skills. Fast readers often comprehend poorly; slow readers often comprehend well. To say that speed alone, or comprehension alone, is the measure of a skilled reader is to have adopted a particular conceptual stance that has not, when looking at the entirety of brain research, been supported. At the beginning of the twentieth century, one of the most respected early thinkers about reading, Edmund Huey, told us that, "... to completely analyze what we do when we read would almost be the acme of a psychologist's achievements, for it would be to describe very many of the most intricate workings of the human's mind" (1906, p. 6).

❝ There is nothing normative about reading. ❞

Describing the most intricate workings of the human's mind is what many are still trying to do. Some connect reading to studying eye movements. Others connect it to studying the role of prior knowledge. Others focus on vocabulary, and still others focus on how the brain figures out letter-sound correspondences. And then even more researchers focus on comprehension strategies. They are all still trying to understand the "most intricate workings of the human's mind."

Space

Perhaps the most important part of reading has little to do with looking at the words. Maybe the most important part of reading happens when we are not reading, during the moments when we pause, look up, and wonder. Perhaps the reading has less to do with the words on the page and more to do with the thoughts in the mind, with the questions we did not even know we had until we entered the text.

> **Maybe the most important part of reading happens when we are not reading, during the moments when we pause, look up, and wonder.**

Yes, we want readers to pay attention to the words on the page, of course, and to read the text closely and carefully. We want readers to respect themselves, their own thoughts and feelings. We want them to laugh, to cry, to hold their collective breath as they anticipate what might happen next. We want them to want to read because they just want to enjoy an adventurous adventure or a mysterious mystery. And we want readers to be responsible, to take the reading experience to heart, to let it be significant in their intellectual and emotional lives. But as we reflected on the student who said, "You read it and so what?," we worried he had not been given the permission to stare into space while reading to wonder about his own "So what?"

Reading and Rereading

Early on in children's reading lives, the *So what?* becomes "what's next?" Children want a book like one they've just finished, or, at a very young age, they want the same book again. And again.

Toddlers voice their "what's next" at first with a delighted plea to "read it again." After the millionth time, though, you don't give a damn where that red balloon is as you read, "Goodnight moon. Goodnight room. Goodnight red balloon" in Margaret Wise Brown's beloved *Goodnight Moon.* We want them to move on to *The Red Balloon* by Anthony Clark or *Red Shoes* by Karen English or anything other than that one book! But they start with rereading.

For a long while (if we would let them), kids read to enjoy the plot, then the character. It's later that they want to consider theme. We could avoid our student's dismayed, "I read it and so what?," if we'd let them read voraciously what they *want* to read for as long as they want to read it. Yes, that means there is nothing wrong with a child wanting *Bedtime for Frances* (required reading nightly by one of Kylene's kids for far longer than Kylene cared whether Frances ever went to bed or not) or *The Big Book of Why* (required reading by her other one). There is nothing wrong if a middle-schooler wants to read *Flooded: Requiem for Johnstown* three times in one month or a high school student keeps returning to *Hidden Figures*. What those students are doing during those rereadings is wondering and wandering. There is, however, a lot wrong with teachers spending four to six weeks reading and studying one book. Who wants to spend six weeks on one book?

> **"We want children to fall head over heels in love with reading so that when the reading gets tough—and it will—they have developed the stamina to stick with it."**

We fear that the statement we shared earlier, "I read it and so what?" came from a child much too young to have given up on reading. It came from a child who had learned to equate reading with finishing some task. We want children to fall head over heels in love with reading so that when the reading gets tough—and it will—they have developed the stamina to stick with it. No one starts kids playing sports by making them do two-a-days in the August heat. No, they start with the fun of tossing a ball or watching a game on TV with the family. They fall in love with the sport and then they begin to develop nuanced skills. No one would ever take away the high school football coach (well, at least not in Texas or Florida, our home states) because the football players are now in high school and have been learning the game since they were six. No. That's when they hire the most coaches because the game has gotten harder. And why are the kids willing to keep working harder? Because part of the *So what?* is that they love the game.

So, let your kids read and reread all the *Frog and Toad* books they want. Those books are showing them something about friendship, sharing, forgiveness, courage—something that's speaking to them. Hand them yet another *I Survived* book. Maybe they just love the adventure; perhaps they are testing themselves against the main character; maybe they are wondering about their own chances of surviving some catastrophe they have imagined. Let them read *The Cruisers*, or *Jasmine Toguchi*. Hand them Kwame Alexander's *The Crossover* and all his others. They might have started with Sharon Draper's series *Clubhouse Mysteries* and then moved on to *Stella by Starlight* and *Blended*. They might have read one Jacqueline Woodson or Matt de la Peña or Chris Crutcher or Carlos Hernandez, Jason Reynolds, Andrew Smith or . . . the list (thankfully) goes on and on and then said, simply, "Could I have more, please?" Or, as one student said after reading *Stotan!* by Chris Crutcher, "He's pretty good. I guess if you have to read, he's a good one to read. Got another?" For a ninth grader who had made it his goal to not read any books that year, we thought this was high praise. But through all those books, they were discovering that the most important "So what?" is answered with "because it meant something to me."

> **At some point, they aren't simply lost in a good story, but are getting found.**

Often, as Smith and Wilhelm (2002; 2013) point out, students get impatient with the task of reading because it doesn't seem to lead to practical results. Once they have read, they want to be able to bake the cake or fix the car. For those readers, the "So what?" lies in a practical purpose, and there is nothing wrong with that. Those are our kids who read to figure out something specific, and they are the ones to whom interests are critically important as we help them decide what they want to read. These are the students who already read with the BHH-D framework in mind.

The more subtle, but critically important, things they might do after they read—change their minds about human relations, about their responsibilities in the society or the world, about who they are and what they value—often come later in their development.

But their willingness to do that more sophisticated thinking begins with laughing at the early antics in *Captain Underpants*, a series that ends with *Captain Underpants and the Sensational Saga of Sir Stinks-A-Lot* revealing that a main character, Harold, has married a man. This matter-of-fact presentation, made with no drama and no commentary, gives students the chance to recognize that this author thought there was nothing momentous in this event. They got married. End of story. As students read Sharon Draper's *Jericho* series, they figure out how they might cope with the peer pressure. They think about identity with Matt de la Peña's *Mexican WhiteBoy* and Bill Konigsberg's *The Music of What Happens*. At some point, they aren't simply lost in a good story, but are getting found. They wonder about questions such as:

- What does this mean to me?

- What does it say about my place in the world?

- Do I need to ask some questions, explore some uncertainties?

- Do I need to read something else, perhaps with a different perspective?

- Do I need to change some attitudes or beliefs?

- Do I need to change some behavior or take some action?

- Do I need to try to influence those around us, perhaps try to reshape the world slightly?

- Do I need to act? Am I ready to do something, to change something?

Younger readers' wondering questions might appear more as statements, not yet having developed the abstract thinking that allows introspective verbal statements. You might hear them say or ask:

- This made me happy/sad/worried/afraid.

- They weren't being nice.

- I wouldn't do that.

- I like my friends because they are nice.

- No one should bully others.

- Why did that character do that?

- Why does that person act that way?

- How can we fix this?

- I want another book like this.

At whatever age and whatever stage, our young student was right. If we read it and then there is no "So what?" worth exploring, then why did we read? If we don't give the time to do some wondering and some wandering, then we have not given students the time to become the empowered thinkers we desperately need them to be. The smith can't forge the metal into a piece of art without time. The potter can't shape the clay into art without time. Change takes time. And of course it means having books. This chart shows that even as kids read less throughout their education, a classroom library makes a positive difference.

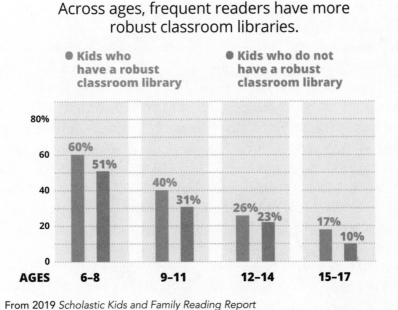

From 2019 *Scholastic Kids and Family Reading Report*

18

Forging Ahead

IN MID-JUNE OF 2020, SOME PEOPLE GASPED IN horror when a statue of Francis Scott Key, author of the national anthem, *The Star-Spangled Banner*, was toppled and destroyed. They called this a "despicable act."

We know two of those people, two white people. We wondered if they did not know, or knew at one time and forgot, who Key really was. He was more than an amateur poet who penned a poem one night.

Key was a rich slave owner, a friend of President Andrew Jackson, and as strong a supporter of slavery as the President. As district attorney in the Washington, D.C., area, Key worked hard to uphold current slavery laws and enact new ones. If he were to be described, as some slave owners were, as a "benevolent slave master," that phrase should evoke the same horror as hearing that someone is a "gentle rapist."

When Jackson became President, Key encouraged him to make his brother-in-law, Roger B. Taney, another rich slave owner, the Chief Justice of the Supreme Court. Jackson complied and the pro-slavery movement had another strong voice in its corner. It was Taney's court that heard the famous Dred Scott case. Taney wrote the majority opinion that denied Scott, a Black man who had paid for his freedom,

SUPREME COURT OF THE UNITED STATES,

DECEMBER TERM, 1856.

DRED SCOTT

versus

JOHN F. A. SANDFORD.

DRED SCOTT, PLAINTIFF IN ERROR, *v.* JOHN F. A. SANDFORD.

I.

1. Upon a writ of error to a Circuit Court of the United States, the transcript of the record of all the proceedings in the case is brought before this court, and is open to its inspection and revision.

2. When a plea to the jurisdiction, in abatement, is overruled by the court upon demurrer, and the defendant pleads in bar, and upon these pleas the final judgment of the court is in his favor—if the plaintiff brings a writ of error, the judgment of the court upon the plea in abatement is before this court, although it was in favor of the plaintiff—and if the court erred in overruling it, the judgment must be reversed, and a mandate issued to the Circuit Court to dismiss the case for want of jurisdiction.

3. In the Circuit Courts of the United States, the record must show that the case is one in which by the Constitution and laws of the United States, the court had jurisdiction—and if this does not appear, and the court gives judgment either for plaintiff or defendant, it is error, and the judgment must be reversed by this court—and the parties cannot by consent waive the objection to the jurisdiction of the Circuit Court.

4. A free negro of the African race, whose ancestors were brought to this country and sold as slaves, is not a "citizen" within the meaning of the Constitution of the United States.

5. When the Constitution was adopted, they were not regarded in any of the States as members of the community which constituted the State, and were not numbered among its "people or citizens." Consequently, the special rights and immunities guarantied to citizens do not apply to them. And not being "citizens" within the meaning of the Constitution, they are not entitled to sue in that character in a court of the United States; and the Circuit Court has not jurisdiction in such a suit.

6. The only two clauses in the Constitution which point to this race, treat them as persons whom it was morally lawful to deal in as articles of property and to hold as slaves.

7. Since the adoption of the Constitution of the United States, no state can by any subsequent law make a foreigner or any other description of persons citizens of the United States, nor entitle them to the rights and privileges secured to citizens by that instrument.

8. A State, by its laws passed since the adoption of the Constitution, may put a foreigner or any other description of persons upon a footing with its own citizens, as to all the rights and privileges enjoyed by them within its dominion, and by its laws. But that will not make him a citizen of the United States, nor entitle him to sue in its courts, nor to any of the privileges and immunities of a citizen in another State.

9. The change in public opinion and feeling in relation to the African race, which has taken place since the adoption of the Constitution, cannot change its construction and meaning, and it must be construed and administered now according to its true meaning and intention when it was formed and adopted.

10. The plaintiff having admitted, by his demurrer to the plea in abatement, that his ancestors were imported from Africa and sold as slaves, he is not a citizen of the State of Missouri according to the Constitution of the United States, and was not entitled to sue in that character in the Circuit Court.

11. This being the case, the judgment of the court below, in favor of the plaintiff on the plea in abatement, was erroneous.

that freedom he was due, and went further, saying that "all people of African descent free or slave, were not United States citizens and therefore had no right to sue in federal court" (*Dred Scott v. Sanford*). Key's work as an attorney enforcing slave laws and his encouragement to appoint Taney to the Supreme Court makes his line in the anthem "Home of the free and land of the brave" mean less or makes it meaningless. He did not want all men to be free. He did not see all men as equal. He saw white men as free and Black men (and women) as not equal and therefore undeserving of freedom.

We asked these people who called the act of removing Key's statue "despicable" why any person would want anyone to think that he deserves a statue. As they considered what we had told them about Key, they responded, "Oh, I didn't know that. Toppling it over seems wrong but keeping it up is wrong. I don't know."

"Oh, I didn't know that." There is so much we do not know. But once we know, we must be better and do better. Their admission that "I don't know [what to do]" is a small step forward. But it is a step forward, and it is not silence. None of us can live in the false security of silence any longer. To stay silent about wrong acts is to speak loudly. Instead, with love and encouragement, with sincerity and strength, with hope and humility, we must offer a voice that rings loudly a true version of who we have been in this nation and sings a better song of who it is we might become. And, as is so often the case, our young people are leading the way.

These are their names:

Sonita Alizadeh	Jaclyn Corin	Iqbal Masih
Sophie Cruz	David Hogg	Claudette Colvin
Melati & Isabel Wijsen	Emma González	Bana al-Abed
Jazz Jennings	Yara Shahidi	Anoyara Khatun
Payal Jangid	Jamie Margolin	Nkosi Johnson
Marley Dias	Isra Hirsi	Thandiwe Chama
Kelvin Doe	Mari Copeny	Alex Scott
Malala Yousafzai	Autumn Peltier	Yash Gupta
Jack Andraka	Bruno Rodriguez	Jade Fuller
Katie Eder	Helena Gualinga	Nya Collins
Blair Imani	Nicholas Lowinger	Zee Thomas
Greta Thunberg	Jaylen Arnold	Kennedy Green
Alex Wind	Jahkil Jackson	Emma Rose Smith
Cameron Kasky	Ryan Hickman	Mikayla Smith
	Zuriel Oduwole	

Top (left to right): Malala Yousafzai, Jahkil Jackson, Greta Thunberg, Sophie Cruz
Bottom (left to right): David Hogg, Sonita Alizadeh, Marley Dias

Perhaps you recognize some of those names—Jazz, Greta, Emma, Malala. Perhaps in recognizing a few, you understood the list. These are names of child or teen activists from around the world. These are the names of kids who decided to do something. These are kids who are changing the world.

Let us tell you about a few.

Sonita Alizadeh is a teenage Afghan rapper who uses her music to fight child marriage. Sophie Cruz, from Mexico, advocates for immigrants' rights. Melati and Isabel Wijsen created the Bye-Bye Plastic Bags program for Bali in 2013 when they were 12 and 10 years old, respectively. In 2018, Bali was declared plastic-bag free, and now Indonesia, following their same plan, hopes to be plastic-bag free by 2021.

Marley Dias started the #1000BlackGirlBooks when she was eleven.

Alex Wind, Cameron Kasky, Jaclyn Corin, David Hogg, and Emma González are the Parkland teens who are working to end gun violence in the United States. Mari Copeny is a water activist from Flint, Michigan. Nicholas Lowinger started the Gotta Have Sole movement that encourages people to donate shoes to kids in homeless shelters.

Jahkil Jackson was nine when he started giving out Orange Blessing Bags for the homeless.

Iqbal Masih, from Pakistan, escaped slavery at age 10 and went on to help 3,000 more children to escape. He was assassinated at age 12.

Alex Scott started a lemonade stand when he was five years old. His goal was to help fight cancer. His first stand raised $2,000. He had helped raise $1,000,000 for cancer research before he died. Now Alex's Lemonade Stand Foundation has raised over $150,000,000.

Jade Fuller, Nya Collins, Zee Thomas, Kennedy Green, Emma Rose Smith, and Mikayla Smith are the six teenage girls from Nashville, Tennessee, who are all between 14 and 16 years old at the time of this writing. They were the ones who organized the peaceful Nashville Black Lives Matter march on June 4, 2020, to protest the police killings of Black men and women. Over 15,000 people attended.

We don't know who these very young people will be when they grow up. We know that some already haven't lived to grow up. But we know that Maya Angelou, Barbara Gittings, Frederick Douglass, Nikki Giovanni, Langston Hughes, Louis Braille, Elizabeth Acevedo, Louise Rosenblatt, Paulo Freire, Wynton Marsalis, Mahatma Gandhi, Mother Teresa, Louis Pasteur, Florence Nightingale, Colin Kaepernick, Tommie Smith, Pedro Noguera, John Carlos, Congressman John Lewis, Harvey Milk, President Barack Obama, Madeleine Albright, Dorothy Vaughan, Congresswoman Sharice Davids, Martin Luther King, Jr., Katherine Johnson, Julia Alvarez, Alexandria Ocasio-Cortez, Isabel Campoy, Harriet Tubman, Alma Flor Ada, Sojourner Truth, Ahmed Zewail, Albert Einstein, Keith Harper, Melba Pattillo Beals, Ellen DeGeneres, Hoda Kotb, Jacqueline Woodson, Ibram X. Kendi, and so many others were all kids once. All kids who sat in someone's classroom, who sat at a table or desk. Some were their own teachers. But all learned to read and to write.

Those were their tools: reading and writing. And with those tools they forged a life that endeavored to create a better life for us all, the same as so many young people are doing today.

CONCLUSION

What We've Known All Along

WE'VE KNOWN THIS ALL ALONG, OR AT LEAST SOME did. But in that knowing, some have fought against it, taught around it, and flatly rejected understanding it in many ways. Perhaps that is because we jumped in too quickly, all of us, to teach the skills of it, without understanding the power of this *it*. And in all that jumping, we mangled it. Now it's time we undo the damage done and decide to not allow this damage to happen again.

What's the *this*, the *it*? That literacy is power. The ability to read brings with it power and privilege; depriving anyone of literacy amounts to denying them power. It is an act of suppression.

We've analyzed reading. Dissected reading. We've studied eye movements, eye fixations, rate of reading, rate of pausing. We've taught decoding through onset-rime, phonics, whole words, look-see. We've put children into groups labeled according to bird colors (red birds and blue birds) or alphabet letters ("I'll meet with the H readers today"). We've Lexiled, DIBELed (or, is it DIBELLed?), and leveled texts. And we've introduced kids to round-robin reading, choral-reading, popcorn reading, guided reading, and silent reading. We've taught kids a strategy for everything—so many strategies, in fact, that they probably don't how to apply them to anything.

They know to turn and talk, stop and jot, and, thanks to us, notice and note. All that's left to do is pause and ponder or hesitate and hypothesize. Or, perhaps, get up and get out. We've grouped, individualized, differentiated, remediated, accelerated, and tolerated texts that informed children that "The rat sat on the mat while wearing a hat" or that "Pop would hop until he would stop and land with a plop." And many of us spent our childhoods learning to read by discovering that Spot could run and that Dick and Jane could play and that Father always wore a suit and Mother cleaned house in a dress.

We've taught kids power words, sight words, high-frequency words, low-frequency words, open-syllable words, closed-syllable words, when all they want to read and say, by this point, are naughty words. We're probably muttering them, too.

Then, weirdly, we wonder, perplexed and then surprised, when we discover year after year after year that more and more children say they don't like to read.

And so we blame. We say kids are distracted by the Internet, by video, by television, by noisy homes, by too much homework, by too many sports, by too much pressure, by . . . anything else we can think of that day. Parents don't care; parents care too much; parents don't support; parents support too much. Mom's not at home; mom is home and hovering. The texts are too easy; the texts are too hard; there's not enough choice; there is too much choice; we don't have enough books; we don't have enough good books; we don't have enough money to buy enough good books. Our books aren't mirrors; our books aren't windows; our community doesn't want kids to read those kinds of books—you know, the ones that show kids something beyond what makes certain parents comfortable. Those parents only want books that reflect the values and customs and society they think is this world, or at least the world they want their kids in. Some educators go straight for kids, saying they don't care. Or, they care too much and only want to read books that will allow them to get the best score on whatever program the district is using that has reduced comprehension to a 90 percent pass rate on a 10-item quiz. Some tell us that kids just won't take the responsibility to even remember to bring their book to class. Or, they take on too much responsibility and are stressed.

Or, we point out that we can't spend time letting kids have discussions because we must get ready for the test.

Ah, yes. The TEST. The test has become the tail that wags the dog. It's all about the test because the test leads to a score and the score leads to ratings of teachers and principals and superintendents and school districts and, ultimately, all the way up to home values and property taxes. The test. *That* test. That damned test.

> **"Reading is the doorway to power. To privilege. To building a mind. To cultivating self-determination."**

And in all of that, we have forgotten something that perhaps some of us never had the time to consider. Reading is the doorway to power. To privilege. To building a mind. To cultivating self-determination. To helping each of us come together to create a society steeped in reason and responsibility and held together by hope and humility. Reading is far more than a window or a mirror. Reading, reading with purpose and passion, with a curious mind and a skeptical eye, is a way to find yourself while crafting yourself; to become independent of manipulation, of control, of a life determined by someone else.

Reading is power.

Our history has, for too long, been the suppression of power.

Reading has, for too long, not risen to the place it should be in our daily lives: those precious moments when we can be both within ourselves and outside ourselves.

You, our nation's teachers, have the power to help students become empowered readers and thinkers. You can help each student forge his or her life through reading. And so, again, dear teachers, we turn to you.

Acknowledgments

AS ALWAYS, OUR BOOKS ARE NOT WRITTEN IN ISOLATION, but represent a compilation of thought accumulated over years and inspired by many. The same is true of this book. Friends, teachers, and colleagues, including Cornelius Minor, Aeriale Johnson, Brent Gilson, Jen Ochoa, Jeff Williams, Ali Aten Rash, Linda Rief, Penny Kittle, Kwame Alexander, Kelly Gallagher, Chad Everett, Ernest Morrell, Pam Allyn, Sharon Draper, Chris Crutcher, Naomi Shihab Nye, Isobel Campoy, Alma Flor Ada, Michael Guevero, Lester Laminack, and Jacqueline Woodson, added their insight.

Our Scholastic family, including Lois Bridges, Ray Coutu, Danny Miller, Sarah Longhi, Tom Martinez, Liana Zamora, Maria Lilja, Greg Worrell, Michael Haggen, and of course, Dick Robinson, supported this book through its many revisions as we wanted "just a little more time" to make sure it was saying what we wanted it to say. Our families, as always, stood by and stood aside as we disappeared for hours at a time to work on this one paragraph or that one. As always, we thank them for their patience and support.

And, with respect and admiration, we acknowledge the critical contributions to this nation by Congressman John Lewis and Supreme Court Associate Justice Ruth Bader Ginsburg. Our nation lost both of these tireless advocates for equity and justice in 2020. They taught us what was right, and now is our time to show we learned their lessons well.

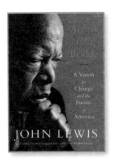

In a 2017 NPR article, Lewis recounted that when he was in school, he "had one teacher who'd tell me over and over again, she would say, 'Read, my child. Read.'" He said he followed her advice and "tried to read everything." It was through all his reading that one day he read a newspaper article about Ruby Bridges, and her life inspired him. That, and a letter he wrote at age 15 to Martin Luther King, Jr., which King answered, forged for him a path of activism.

Justice Ginsburg had a similar relationship with reading and said, "Reading is the key that opens doors to many good things in life." She was right. It is the key. But it is only a key. We must do the turning of that key. We must let the truth of what we read enter our minds and our hearts so that we, too, may be forged by reading. We must cherish the power of a literate life. We must read responsibly, with an eye toward change, and a heart of humility.

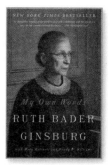

We close our book by acknowledging our nation's teachers. Each day, you do what heroes do: you show up and you stand ready for all there is yet to do.

Until we elect local, state, and national lawmakers who are not racists, not homophobic, not misogynistic, not bought by special-interest groups; until we learn that blindly accepting the views of the talk-radio/news-show political pundits without understanding the issues means giving up our own thinking; until we recognize that the reading and writing we do in schools should prepare us to question, to wonder, to grow, and to change, not merely to pass a test; until this nation stands together demanding equity for all, then our democracy will be at risk and your job will remain harder than we ever thought possible. And you will need to be brave. You will need to be brave as you stand against all that would make your teaching less.

We write the books we write—this one in particular—because we believe that one way forward for this nation is through a highly educated citizenry. We want children who think. Who read attentively. Write passionately. Embrace joyfully. Try repeatedly. Question often. Think creatively. Speak thoughtfully. Work collaboratively. Listen compassionately. And change their minds when reason and evidence or empathy and understanding require such a change. We want them to find more

> **66 ...until this nation stands together demanding equity for all, then our democracy will be at risk and your job will remain harder than we ever thought possible. And you will need to be brave. 99**

similarities than differences with those unlike them. We want them to stand boldly, courageously, and steadfastly with those who are bullied, brutalized, and marginalized. We want them to understand that moving from an inspiring moment to a life-changing movement requires urgency, humility, bravery, honesty, and a yearning for justice and equity.

We know the books children read can help them accomplish at least some of those goals. And we hope our books help you accomplish some of those goals, too. We know that without you our nation is at greater risk. But with you, with those of you who are willing to be brave, we know tomorrow will be better.

Appendix A:
Explanation of the
Notice & Note Signposts

In *Notice and Note: Strategies for Close Reading* and *Reading Nonfiction: Notice & Note Stances, Signposts, and Strategies,* we shared that we had noticed, in both fiction and nonfiction, recurring moves authors made—what we could call the author's craft. We thought that an awareness of these moves would help readers, while reading fiction, to understand the author's theme, and while reading nonfiction, to understand the author's purpose or bias. We called these moves *signposts.* Our idea was that if we could teach students to notice these signposts, take note of them, and then ask themselves one question about them—the anchor question—then we would be moving students closer to becoming independent close readers. As such readers, they would be less reliant on what teachers told them to notice and which questions they were to answer and more reliant on their own abilities to notice critical elements and then question the texts themselves.

Here we'll offer you one example of a fiction signpost and one example of a nonfiction signpost.

Example of a Fiction Signpost

One of the fiction signposts reminds students to look for places in the text (or illustrations) where the author shows us a character or characters acting in a way we wouldn't expect or in a way the character had not acted before. Recognizing this contrast with our own expectations or change in behavior helps students understand character development, which will eventually help students realize the theme. We call this signpost Contrast and Contradiction, and we tell students that when they notice this, they should ask themselves, "I wonder why the character is acting this way?"

Here's how this might look in a third-grade classroom. We had told the students that authors show us how characters change in a book by letting them act in different ways. Third graders remembered that when they were "young," some sucked their thumb but now that they are "old," they don't. They immediately saw that their change in action meant they were changing. We told them when they noticed a character changing in a book, it would be called a Contrast and Contradiction. Then we told them they should ask themselves, "What does this make me wonder about?" Because these students were very young, we used that easier anchor question. Had they been older, we would have introduced them to an anchor question that pushes harder on character development: "Why does the character act this way?"

Then we showed them the book we would be reading aloud, *The Other Side* by Jacqueline Woodson. We asked what they noticed and told them to turn and talk with a partner. After a moment, they shared. Some said they noticed that there were two girls. Others noticed the fence. But one group said, "We noticed a Contrast and Contradiction. It's like they are looking at each other but they aren't playing with each other. That made us wonder why they aren't playing together? Is it because they can't climb the fence like your mom says don't go across the street or is it because one is Black and one is white?" One Black student said, "I noticed that the Black girl is the main girl, like she is the bigger one and that seemed different to me because most of our picture story books have white people as the main characters."

Notice that we did not ask students to look at the cover and make a prediction. We've all done that before and from that we probably would have received answers that focused on plot, perhaps: "We think that the two girls aren't friends now but will become friends by the end of the book." Asking them to look at the Contrast and Contradiction signpost focused their attention on how the characters might act and what the problem— conflict—might be.

For middle and high school teachers, we read this story with students who are beginning to read books on equity and social justice. As they looked at the cover, their comments were similar but reflected the maturity we'd expect of older students:

> Ninth grader: "I see a Contrast and Contradiction because the white girl is up on the fence, which is dividing them, but the Black girl is not. Maybe that's just because the Black girl has a swing and the white girl doesn't, but it also made me wonder if at this time white people didn't worry about boundaries as much as Black people had to worry about them."

Eleventh grader: "The fence is obviously there to keep them apart, probably a metaphor for segregation. But the contrast is that they are looking at each other. If they were adults, they probably would not be. This makes me think that there's going to be a theme that it will be teens and young people who change everything, not adults."

On the following page you will find a chart that introduces you to the fiction signposts and offers the anchor question we would have students ask of themselves once they notice the signpost.

Example of a Nonfiction Signpost

One of the nonfiction signposts we always teach students is Numbers and Stats. While easy to notice—look for numerals or words that represent amounts, such as "many," "few," "a lot," or "all"—this signpost is often overlooked. Students (or adults) don't pause to ask themselves why the author chose to offer a specific number or left the number vague. Here's a passage we share with older students (and teachers in workshops) to ask them to consider the numbers and stats they see in this passage and chart and discuss their implications:

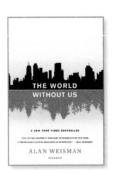

Worldwide, every four days human population rises by 1 million. Since we can't really grasp such numbers, they'll wax out of control until they crash, as has happened to every other species that got too big for this box. About the only thing that could change that, short of the species-wide sacrifice of voluntary human extinction, is to prove that intelligence really makes us special after all. The intelligent solution would require the courage and the wisdom to put our knowledge to the test. It would be poignant and distressing in ways, but not fatal. It would henceforth limit every human female on Earth capable of bearing children to one (Weisman, pp. 347–8).

The following is a short conversation about that passage from three tenth graders, students the teacher had assured us would not be involved in the conversation: "It's almost the end of the year and they have really checked out." They had been told to read the passage and then discuss the numbers

Fiction Signposts	Anchor Questions
Contrast and Contradiction These are sharp contrasts between what we expect and what we see the character actually doing. You'll spot these moments by being alert for times in which the character does something that isn't what you expect him to do.	**For primary grade students:** *What does this make me wonder about?* **For older students:** *Why would the character act or feel this way?*
Aha/Epiphany Moment This is the moment when a character realizes something about her situation or her problem. Watch for phrases such as "I understood" or "I realized" or "I figured out" or "I finally knew" as a signal to an Aha Moment.	**For primary grade students:** *What does this make me wonder about?* **For older students:** *How might this change things?*
Tough Questions These are the very difficult questions the character asks himself. You'll notice these questions because they are often questions the main character asks himself or a trusted friend. Sometimes these appear as "I wonder" statements.	**For primary grade students:** *What does this make me wonder about?* **For older students:** *What does this question make me wonder about?*
Words of the Wiser This is the advice or insight a wiser, usually older, character offers the main character to help guide her through her difficulties. Be alert for scenes in which a character—who often is older—offers advice to the main character.	**For primary grade students:** *What does this make me wonder about?* **For older students:** *What's the life lesson and how might it affect the character?*
Again and Again These are events, images, situations, or even just words or phrases, that come up over and over in a story, often separated by many pages. These symbolic moments help reveal information about characters, conflict, and plot. You have to be alert for something that is repeated. Sometimes the repetition happens within a few pages, but other times it might be a few chapters.	**For primary grade students:** *What does this make me wonder about?* **For older students:** *Why might the author bring this up again and again?*
Memory Moment This is the moment when a character tells us about a memory of something from his past. This is not a flashback, which interrupts the forward momentum of the narrative. Phrases such as "I remembered" or "This reminded me of" or "This was like the time that" or "The memory of this" show you the character is having a Memory Moment. These moments usually explain character motivation or plot progression.	**For primary grade students:** *What does this make me wonder about?* **For older students:** *Why might this memory be important?*

and stats they had noticed and talk about why the author used those numbers.

Student 1: One million more people every four days?

Student 2: So, in 8 days, like just a week, two million people?

Student 3: Does it say where? Like is this just here? Where it is?

Student 1: Here's another number: every female can only have one kid. Really like two numbers because it is "every" and it is "one."

Student 3: I don't think you can tell women how many kids they can have.

Student 2: So, how do you make this a law? What if someone didn't want to follow it but was against abortion.

Student 1: This would be like legalizing abortion? What would the anti-abortion people say?

Student 3: Didn't they do this in China?

Student 1: But maybe to save the world because you can't keep adding millions then we have to do this.

Student 2: Do people know this? Is this real? Is this like now?

Kids who had checked out, checked back in quickly. Why? First, as one told us, "It was easier to talk about this because we knew we had to look for Numbers and Stats. But I hadn't ever asked myself stuff about numbers before. You see the numbers and that's it. But when you know to think about them, then you have all these other questions in mind." Second, it was a topic that became interesting to them so they began generating their own questions. Once students begin generating questions, then they are making it relevant. And remember, rigor without relevance is simply hard.

What follows is a chart that introduces you to the nonfiction signposts and offers the anchor question we would have students ask of themselves once they notice the signpost.

Nonfiction Signposts	Anchor Questions
Contrast and Contradiction The author shows a sharp contrast between things/people/ideas; a contradiction between one element in the text and another; or a contrast between what is presented and what you know or believe.	**For younger students:** *What does this make me wonder about?* **For older students:** *What is the difference and why does it matter?*
Extreme or Absolute Language The author states something absolutely, uncompromisingly, extravagantly. Perhaps the statement is, or appears to be, exaggerated.	**For younger students:** *What does this make me wonder about?* **For older students:** *Why did the author use this language?*
Numbers and Stats The author uses numbers, perhaps statistics, or perhaps words that indicate amount ("a huge number," "very few") to make some point.	**For younger students:** *What does this make me wonder about?* **For older students:** *Why does the author share these numbers?*
Quoted Words The author quotes or cites someone else. In other situations, the author makes a statement that should be attributed to someone but fails to cite a source.	**For younger students:** *What does this make me wonder about?* **For older students:** *Why did the author quote or cite someone else? Why did the author fail to mention the source? What did this add to his argument?*
Word Gaps The author has used a word or a phrase that you don't know.	**For all students:** *Do I know this word in another context? Does the word seem to be a technical word? Are there clues in the sentence that might help me understand the word?*

Appendix B:
Grant Opportunities for Books and Building Inclusive Libraries

If you are looking to build your classroom library, or to make it more inclusive, take a look at any of the following sites:

- www.adoptaclassroom.org/tag/grants-for-diverse-books/
- www.ezra-jack-keats.org/section/ezra-jack-keats-mini-grant-program-for-public-libraries-public-schools/
- www.believeinreading.org
- www.readacrossamerica.org/free-books-for-kids-classrooms/
- www.readbrightly.com/
- diversebooks.org/
- www.whatdowedoallday.com/books-for-kids/
- www.ala.org/booklists.yalsa.net/
- www.booksource.com/inclusive-classroom-library-checklist%EF%BB%BF
- diversebooks.org/resources/where-to-find-diverse-books/
- booklovefoundation.org/apply
- www.nehs.us/scholarships-awards/grants/
- snapdragonbookfoundation.org/
- www.laurabushfoundation.com/
- www.dgliteracy.org/grant-programs/
- bookfairs.scholastic.com/bookfairs/landing-page.html
- bookfairs.scholastic.com/bookfairs/articles/catalog.html
- www.halfpricebooks.com/book-donations-request-form/

References

https://www.nytimes.com/2019/12/19/learning/what-students-are-saying-about-how-to-improve-american-education.html

https://www.theatlantic.com/politics/archive/2017/09/trump-urges-nfl-owners-to-fire-players-who-protest/540897/

https://www.msn.com/en-us/sports/motorsports/nascar-bans-any-display-of-confederate-flags-at-races/ar-BB15jooG

Adams, Marilyn. 2006. The Promise of Automatic Speech Recognition for Fostering Literacy Growth in Children and Adults. In the edited volume *International Handbook of Literacy and Technology*, Volume 2. Mahwah, NJ: Lawrence Erlbaum Associates.

Allen, Steve. 1978. *Meeting of Minds*. Los Angeles, New York: Hubris House; distributed by Crown Publishers.

Anderson, Richard C., Paul T. Wilson, and Linda G. Fielding. 1988. Growth in Reading and How Children Spend Their Time Outside of School. *Reading Research Quarterly*, 23, 285–303.

Associated Press. 2020. Trump Tours, Touts Honeywell Mask Factory in Arizona – but Doesn't Wear Mask. *U.S. & World*. Accessed at https://www.syracuse.com/us-news/2020/05/trump-tours-touts-honeywell-mask-factory-in-arizona-but-doesnt-wear-mask.htm

Baldrige, Letitia. 1993. *Complete Guide to Executive Manners*. New York: Scribner, p. 52.

Baldwin, James. 1960. They Can't Turn Back. Accessed at http://www.historyisaweapon.com/defcon1/baldwincantturnback.html

Beers, Kylene and Robert E. Probst. 2014. *Notice & Note: Strategies for Close Reading*. Portsmouth, NH: Heinemann.

Beers, Kylene and Robert E. Probst. 2016. *Reading Nonfiction: Notice & Note Stances, Signposts, and Strategies*. Portsmouth, NH: Heinemann.

Beers, Kylene and Robert E. Probst. 2017. *Disrupting Thinking: Why How We Read Matters*. Portsmouth, NH: Heinemann.

Beers, Kylene, Robert E. Probst and Linda Rief. 2007. *Adolescent Literacy: Turning Promise into Practice*. Portsmouth, NH: Heinemann.

Beers, Kylene. 2002. *When Kids Can't Read, What Teachers Can Do: A Guide for Teachers*. Portsmouth, NH: Heinemann.

Bishop, Rudine Sims. 1990. "Mirrors, Windows, and Sliding Glass Doors" *Perspectives: Choosing and Using Books for the Classroom*. Vol. 6, no. 3. Summer 1990.

Bridges, Lois and Richard Robinson. 2014. *Open a World of Possible: Real Stories About the Joy and Power of Reading*. New York: Scholastic.

Brief of National Lawyers Guild, and American Civil Liberties Union, Amici Curiae; 10/01/1945; Civil Case File 4292; Gonzalo Mendez et al v. Westminster School District of Orange County et al, 3/2/1945–7/18/1947; Civil Case Files, 1938–1995; Records of District Courts of the United States, Record Group 21; National Archives at Riverside, Perris, CA. Accessed at https://www.docsteach.org/documents/document/brief-nlg-aclu/

Buff, Elizabeth. 2017. Can We Solve World Hunger and Feed 9 Billion People Just by Eating Less Meat?. Accessed at https://www.onegreenplanet.org/environment/world-hunger-population-growth-ditching-meat/

Coates, Ta-Nehisi. (2020). "Ta-Nehisi Coates in *Vanity Fair's* September Issue, The Great Fire." Accessed at https://www.vanityfair.com/culture/2020/08/Ta-Nehisi-Coates-Editor-Letter

Cornelius, Janet Duitsman. 2015. "Slave Testimony: 'We Slipped and Learned to Read'". *A Community of Voices on Education and the African American Experience: A Record of Struggles and Triumphs*. Ervin, Hazel Arnett, and Lois Jamison Sheer. Cambridge: Cambridge Scholars Publishing, p. 43.

Coughlan, Sean. 2017. "10 Toughest Places for Girls to Go to School." BBC News. Accessed at https://www.bbc.com/news/business-41558486

Csikszentmihalyi, Mihaly. 1990. *Flow: The Psychology of Optimal Experience*. New York: Harper & Row.

Daniels, Nicole. 2019. "What Students Are Saying about How to Improve American Education." The New York Times. Accessed at https://www.nytimes.com/2019/12/19/learning/what-students-are-saying-about-how-to-improve-american-education.htlm

Fine, Sarah M. 2019. "I Was a White Teacher Who Couldn't Talk About Race. A Journey through Successful U.S. High Schools Changed My Thinking." Accessed at www.chalkbeat.org

Fischer, Steven Roger. 2019. *A History of Reading*. London, England: Reaction Books, Ltd.

Freire, Paulo. 1970. *Pedagogy of the Oppressed*. New York: Herder and Herder.

Golden, Marita, ed. 2011. *The Word: Black Writers Talk About the Transformative Power of Reading and Writing*. New York: Random House.

Harari, Yuval Noah. 2015. *Sapiens: A Brief History of Humankind*. New York: HarperCollins.

Healey, Jack. 1991. "Jack Healey Talks With Trumpeter Wynton Marsalis About the Good Works of Good Jazz, America's Classical Music." *Spin*. November: 80–82. Print.

HorseChief, Daniel. 2020. Information about Sequoyah. Private email between Dan HorseChief and Kylene Beers, August 17, 2020.

Jones, Van. 2018. *Beyond the Messy Truth: How We Came Apart, How We Come Together*. New York: Ballantine Books.

Kahneman, Daniel. 2013. *Thinking, Fast and Slow*. New York: Farrar, Straus and Giroux.

Kelly, Brian. Sept 2, 2020. "School Decides to Read Book on Black Astronaut to All Students After Parent Complains About It." KMOX News Radio 1120. Accessed at https://kmox.radio.com/articles/news/school-responds-to-complaint-about-book-on-black-astronaut.

Kendi, Ibram X. 2016. *Stamped from the Beginning: The Definitive History of Racist Ideas in America*. New York: Nation Books.

Kendi, Ibram X. 2019. *How to Be an Antiracist*. New York: One World.

Knox, Bernard M. W. 1968. *Silent Reading in Antiquity*. Accessed at https://grbs.library.duke.edu/article/view/10731

Knox, Henry. 1789. "To George Washington from Henry Knox, 7 July 1789," *Founders Online*, National Archives, https://founders.archives.gov/documents/Washington/05-03-02-0067

Kraul, Chris. 2005. Vampire Prey on Panama. *Tribune Newspapers: Los Angeles Times*. May 27. Accessed at https://www.latimes.com/archives/la-xpm-2005-may-18-fg-bats18-story.htm

Lindeman, Scarlett. 2018. Chef Enrique Olvera Redefines Mexican Food. Accessed at https://www.cnn.com/travel/article/enrique-olvera-mexico-city/index.html

MacDonald, Victoria-María. 2016. Demanding their Rights: The Latino Struggle for Educational Access and Equity. Washington, D.C., USA: National Parks Service-U.S. Department of the Interior.

Mangan, Dan and Steve Kopak. 2020. Trump Doesn't Wear Coronavirus Mask in Public at Ford Plant. CNBC Politics. Accessed at https://www.cnbc.com/2020/05/21/trump-doesnt-wear-coronavirus-mask-to-ford-plant.html

Marsalis, Wynton. 2020. In *The Economic Other: Inequality in the American Political Imagination.* Condon, Meghan and Amber Wichowsky. Chicago; London: The University of Chicago Press.

McGreevy, Nora. 2020. British Protesters Throw Statue of Slave Trader into Bristol Harbor. *Smithsonian Magazine.* Accessed at https://www.smithsonianmag.com/smart-news/protesters-throw-slavers-statue-bristol-harbor-make-waves-across-britain-180975060/

McWhirter, Cameron. 2011. *Red Summer: The Summer of 1919 and the Awakening of Black America.* New York: Henry Holt & Co.

Mehta, Jal and Sarah M. Fine. 2019. *In Search of Deeper Learning: The Quest to Remake the American High School.* Cambridge, MA: Harvard University Press.

Miller, Eric. 1994. "Washington and the Northwest War, Part One". *George Washington And Indians.* Accessed at http://www.dreric.org/library/northwest.shtlm

Mitchell, Richard. 1979. *Less Than Words Can Say.* Boston: Little, Brown.

Muhammad, Gholdy. 2019. *Cultivating Genius: An Equity Framework for Culturally and Historically Responsive Literacy.* New York: Scholastic.

National Indian Law Library. 1969. Indian Education: A National Tragedy–A National Challenge. 1969. 1969 Report of the Committee on Labor and Public Welfare, United States Senate made by its special subcommittee on Indian Education Pursuant to s. Res. 80. accessed at https://narf.org/nill/resources/education/reports/kennedy/toc.html

Oliver, Stephanie Stokes. 2018. *Black Ink.* New York: Simon and Schuster, Inc.

Postman, Neil. 1985. *Amusing Ourselves to Death: Public Discourse in the Age of Show Business.* New York: Viking.

Probst, Robert E. 1986. "Mom, Wolfgang, and Me: Adolescent Literature, Critical Theory, and the English Classroom." *English Journal 75(6):* 33–39. October.

Probst, Robert E. 2001. "Adolescent Literature and the Teaching of Literature." *Instructional Practices for Literacy Teacher-Educators.* Many, Joyce E. Mahwah, NJ: Lawrence Erlbaum Associates: 159–168.

Probst, Robert E. 2001. "Difficult Days, Difficult Texts." *Voices from the Middle 9(2):* 50–53. December.

Probst, Robert E. 2004, 1988. *Response and Analysis: Teaching Literature in Secondary School.* Portsmouth, NH: Heinemann.

Probst, Robert E. In press. *The Perspicacious Reader: Improving the Capacity for Perspicacity in Pupils of Limited Loquacity While Perusing Puzzling Prose of Perplexing Opacity.* Probst Perspicacity Press: Marathon, FL.

Rasmussen, Birgit B. 1970. "'Attended with Great Inconveniences:' Slave Literacy and the 1740 South Carolina Negro Act" in *The Statutes at Large of Virginia* (Ed.). New York: Arno. Mangan, Dan and Steve Kopak. 2020. https://www.georgiaarchives.org/documents/Slave_Laws_of_Georgia_1755-1860.pdf.

Roots, Kimberly. 2020. NASCAR Bans Any Display of Confederate Flags at Races. TVLine, MSN Sports. Accessed at https://www.msn.com/en-us/sports/motorsports/nascar-bans-any-display-of-confederate-flags-at-races/ar-BB15jooG

Rosenblatt, Louise M. 1938/1995. *Literature as Exploration (first and fifth editions).* New York: Modern Language Association.

Scholastic Publishers. 2019. *Kids and Family Reading Report.* New York: Scholastic. Accessed at https://www.scholastic.com/readingreport/downloads.html

Scholes, Robert E. 1985. *Textual Power: Literary Theory and the Teaching of English.* New Haven, CT: Yale University Press.

Serwer, Adam. 2017. "Trump's War of Words with Black Athletes." *The Atlantic.* Accessed at https://www.theatlantic.com/politics/archive/2017/09/trump-urges-nfl-owners-to-fire-players-who-protest/540897/

Smith, Michael. W. and Jeffrey Wilhelm. 2002. *Reading Don't Fix No Chevys: Literacy in the Lives of Young Men.* Portsmouth, NH: Heinemann.

Soboroff, Jacob. 2020. *Separated: Inside an American Tragedy.* New York: William Morrow, an imprint of HarperCollins Publishers.

Sotomayor, Sonia and Lulu Delacre. 2018. *Turning Pages: My Life Story.* New York: Philomel Books.

Storr, Will. 2014. *The Unpersuadables: Adventures with the Enemies of Science.* New York: The Overlook Press.

Supreme Court of the United States. U.S. Reports: Plessy v. Ferguson, 163 U.S. 537 (1896). Accessed at https://www.loc.gov/item/usrep163537/

Supreme Court of the United States. 2013. Burwell v. Hobby Lobby. Accessed at https://www.supremecourt.gov/opinions/13pdf/13-354_olp1.pdf/

Tatum, Beverly Daniel. 2017. *"Why Are All the Black Kids Sitting Together in the Cafeteria?": And Other Conversations About Race.* New York: Basic Books.

Treuer, David. 2019. *The Heartbeat of Wounded Knee: Native America from 1890 to the Present.* New York: Riverhead Books.

United States Supreme Court. 1954. History – Brown v. Board of Education. Accessed at https://www.uscourts.gov/educational-resources/educational-activities/history-brown-v-board-education-re-enactment

Way, Niobe, Alisha Ali, Carol Gilligan and Pedro Noguera, Eds. 2018. *The Crisis of Connection: Roots, Consequences, and Solutions.* New York: New York University Press.

Weisman, Alan. 2007. *The World Without Us.* New York: Thomas Dunne Books/St. Martin's Press.

Wilhelm, Jeffrey D., Michael W. Smith and Sharon Fransen. 2014. *Reading Unbound: Why Kids Need to Read What They Want-and Why We Should Let Them.* New York: Scholastic.

Wolf, Maryanne and C. J. Stoodley. 2007. *Proust and the Squid: The Story and Science of the Reading Brain.* New York: HarperCollins.

Wolf, Maryanne. 2016. *Tales of Literacy for the 21st Century.* Oxford, UK: Oxford University Press.

Trade books, Poems, and Short Stories

Aliens for Breakfast. Stephanie Spinner and Jonathan Etra.

All American Boys. Jason Reynolds and Brendan Kiely.

"All Summer in a Day." Ray Bradbury.

American Dirt. Jeanine Cummins.

American Street. Ibi Zoboi.

Bedtime for Frances. Russell Hoban.

Blended. Sharon Draper.

Boy at the Back of the Class, The. Onjali Q. Raúf.

Bully. Patricia Polacco.

Captain Underpants and the Sensational Saga of Sir Stinks-A-Lot (and series). Dav Pilkey.

Chocolate War, The. Robert Cormier.

Chrysanthemum. Kevin Henkes.

Clubhouse Mysteries series. Sharon Draper.

Crossover, The. Kwame Alexander.

Cruisers, The. Walter Dean Myers.

Dreamland Burning. Jennifer Latham.

Enemy Pie. Derek Munson.

Flooded: Requiem for Johnstown. Ann E. Burg.

Frog and Toad series. Arnold Lobel.

Giver, The. Lois Lowry.

Hair Love. Matthew A. Cherry.

Hatchet. Gary Paulsen.

Hate U Give, The. Angie Thomas.

Hidden Figures. Margot Lee Shetterly.
I Survived series. Lauren Tarshis.
Ira Sleeps Over. Bernard Waber.
Jasmine Toguchi: Mochi Queen. Debbi Michiko Florence.
Jericho series. Sharon Draper.
Last Stop on Market Street, The. Matt de la Peña.
"Letters to My Daughters #3." Judith Minty.
Long Walk to Water. A. Linda Sue Park.
Make Way for Ducklings. Robert McCloskey.
Mexican WhiteBoy. Matt de la Peña.
Monster. Walter Dean Myers.
Music of What Happens, The. Bill Konigsberg.

My Hair Is a Garden. Cozbi A. Cabrera.
My Name Is Bilal. Asma Mobin-Uddin.
Narrative of the Life of Frederick Douglass. Douglass, Frederick.
National Geographic Little Kids First Big Book of Why. Amy Shields.
New Kid. Jerry Craft.
Other Side, The. Jacqueline Woodson.
Outsiders. The. S. E. Hinton.
Pet. Akwaeke Emezi.
Red Balloon, The. Anthony Clark.
Red Bird Sings: The Story of Zitkala-Sa. Gina Capaldi.
Red Shoes. Karen English.
Romeo and Juliet. William Shakespeare.

Ron's Big Mission. Rose Blue and Corinne J. Naden.
Separate Is Never Equal: Sylvia Mendez & Her Family's Fight for Desegregation. Duncan Tonatiuh.
Some Girls Are. Courtney Summers.
Speak. Laurie Halse Anderson.
Stella by Starlight. Sharon Draper.
"The Story of Cell Phones." Scholastic.
Stotan! Chris Crutcher.
"Thank You, Ma'm." Langston Hughes.
Thirteen Reasons Why. Jay Asher.
To Kill a Mockingbird. Harper Lee.
Wonder. R. J. Palacio.
Your Name Is a Song. Jamilah Thompkins-Bigelow.

Books and Articles That Influenced Our Thinking

Note: We've included some fiction in this list. We think it's long past due that we recognize that fiction, as well as nonfiction, changes the way we think.

Abouzeid, Rania. 2020. *Sisters of the War.* New York: Scholastic.

Ahmed, Samira. 2019. *Internment.* New York: Little Brown.

Alexander, Kwame. 2019. *The Undefeated.* New York: Versify.

Bal, P. M. and M. Veltkamp. 2013. "How Does Fiction Reading Influence Empathy? An Experimental Investigation on the Role of Emotional Transportation." From *PLoS ONE* 8(1): e55341. doi:10.1371/journal.pone.0055341.

Coates, Ta-Nehisi. 2018. *We Were Eight Years in Power: An American Tragedy.* New York: One World Press.

Crutcher, Chris. 2004. "A Hand Up: Who You Callin' Diverse?" *Voices from the Middle* 12(1): 6–7. September.

Darling-Hammond, Linda., Wei, R. C., Andree, A., Richardson, N., Orphanos, S. 2009. Professional learning in the learning profession: A status report on teacher development in the United States and abroad. Oxford, OH: National Staff Development Council and The School Redesign Network at Stanford University.

Desmond, Matthew. 2016. *Evicted: Poverty and Profit in the American City.* New York: Crown.

Dias, Patrick. 1987. *Making Sense of Poetry: Patterns in the Process.* Winnipeg, Canada: Canadian Council of Teachers of English.

Dirda, Michael. 2006. *Book by Book: Notes on Reading and Life.* New York: Henry Holt.

Draper, Sharon. 2012. *Out of My Mind.* New York: Little, Brown Books for Young Readers.

Francois, Chantal. 2013. Reading Is About Relating: Urban Youths Give Voice to the Possibilities for School Literacy. *Journal of Adolescent & Adult Literacy* 57(2) (pp. 141–149).

Golden, Marita, ed. 2011. *The Word: Black Writers Talk About the Transformative Power of Reading and Writing.* New York: Broadway Paperbacks.

Haidt, Jonathan. 2012. *The Righteous Mind: Why Good People Are Divided by Politics and Religion.* New York: Pantheon Books.

Harari, Yuval N. 2017. *Homo Deus: A Brief History of Tomorrow.* New York: Harper, an imprint of HarperCollins Publishers.

Jackson, Yvette. 2005. "Unlocking the Potential of African American Students: Keys to Reversing Underachievement." *Theory and Practice* 44(3): 302–310. August, 2005.

Jones, Van. 2017. *Beyond the Messy Truth: How We Came Apart; How We Come Together.* New York: Ballantine.

Konigsberg, Bill. 2020. *The Bridge.* New York: Scholastic.

Lopez-Robertson, Julia. 2015. No sabía que tenía valor: Uncovering Latina Mothers' Multiple Literacies. *Journal of Family Strengths,* 15(2).

McWhirter, Cameron. 2012. *Red Summer: The Summer of 1919 and the Awakening of Black America.* New York: St. Martin's Press.

Minor, Cornelius. 2019. *We Got This: Equity, Access, and the Quest to Be Who Our Students Need Us to Be.* Portsmouth, NH: Heinemann.

Morrison, Toni. 1993. *Playing in the Dark: Whiteness and the Literary Imagination.* New York: Vintage Books.

Myers, Miles. 1996. *Changing Our Minds: Negotiating English and Literacy.* Urbana, IL: National Council of Teachers of English.

Nafisi, Azar. 2004. *Reading Lolita in Tehran: A Memoir in Books.* New York: Random House.

Noguera, Pedro. 2008. *The Trouble with Black Boys... And Other Reflections on Race, Equity, and the Future of Public Education.* San Francisco: Jossey-Bass.

Oatley, Keith. 2019. "Human Choices." *Evolutionary Studies in Imaginative Culture* 3(1): 73. https://search.ebscohost.com/login.aspx?direct=true&AuthType=ip,shib&db=edsjsr&AN=edsjsr.esic.3.1.124&site=eds-live&scope=site&custid=gsu1

Paul, Annie Murphy. 2012. "Your Brain on Fiction." *New York Times.* New York: New York Times.

Peña de la, Matt. 2010. *Mexican WhiteBoy.* New York: Ember.

Sánchez, Erika. 2019. *I Am Not Your Perfect Mexican Daughter.* New York: Ember.

Solomon, Andrew. 2012. *Far From the Tree: Parents, Children, and the Search for Identity.* New York: Scribner.

Storr, William. 2015. *The Unpersuadables: Adventures with the Enemies of Science.* New York: Overlook Press.

Tatum, Alfred W. 2005. *Teaching Reading to Black Adolescent Males: Closing the Achievement Gap.* Portland, ME: Stenhouse Publishers.

Ward, Jesmyn. 2017. *Sing, Unburied, Sing.* New York: Scribner.

Index

What we offer here is an abridged index—something we're sure we just created! Our original index was ridiculously long as we listed every page where words such as empowerment, power, suppression of power, democracy, literacy, reading, writing, etc., were used. So, we decided to abridge our index and offer you here the names, terms, and charts and graphs we think you might want help finding a second or third time. Terms referring to race, ethnicity, LBGTQ issues, as well as broader concepts, such as literacy, knowledge, thinking, power, or democracy, are not included because those concepts—if not the actual words—permeate this book.

Publisher/content editor: Lois Bridges
Editorial director: Sarah Longhi
Editor-in-chief: Raymond Coutu
Senior editor: Shelley Griffin
Production editor: Danny Miller
Art directors: Tom Martinez and Liana Zamora
Interior designer: Maria Lilja

Photos ©: cover hammer: jmtphotography/Pexels.com; cover books: Africa Studio/Shutterstock; cover left inside flap, left: Courtesy of Kylene Beers; cover left inside flap, right: Courtesy of Robert E. Probst; cover right inside flap, top: Courtesy of Daniel HorseChief; cover right inside flap, center top: Courtesy of Alison Rash; cover right inside flap, center bottom: Courtesy of London Ladd photo by James Bass; cover right inside flap, bottom: Courtesy of Lulu Delacre photo by © Paul Morigi/HMH; cover inside flaps background: Steve Johnson/Pexels.com; 2: Courtesy of Daniel HorseChief; 6: lev radin/Shutterstock; 7 and throughout: The Noun Project; 10: Alison Rash; 30: Niday Picture Library/Alamy Stock Photo; 35: REUTERS/Alamy Stock Photo; 40: ileana_bt/Shutterstock; 58: Courtesy of Kylene Beers; 60: London Ladd/Painted Words, Inc.; 84 scale : tatianasun/Shutterstock; 84 people icon: Colorlife/Shutterstock; 84 agriculture icons: Rimma Rii/Shutterstock; 98 icons: The Noun Project; 115: Photos courtesy of Kylene Beers and Robert E. Probst; 134: Courtesy of Alison Rash; 161 clock: Kseniia Voropaeva/Shutterstock; 161 books: graphixmania/Shutterstock; 166: Courtesy of University of Kentucky Archives; 176, 178: Courtesy of Alison Rash; 187: Library of Congress; 189 Sophie Cruz: Kobby Dagan/Shutterstock; 189 Jahkil Jackson: MJ Photos/Shutterstock; 189 Greta Thunberg: Stephen Lovekin/Shutterstock; 189 Malala Yousafzai: Fabio De Paola/Shutterstock; 189 David Hogg: MediaPunch/Shutterstock; 189 Sonita Alizadeh: Stephen Lovekin/Shutterstock; 189 Marley Dias: Matt Baron/Shutterstock/Shutterstock.

Pages 47–48: Excerpt from *Aliens for Breakfast* by Jonathan Etra and Stephanie Spinner. Text copyright © 1988 by Jonathan Etra and Stephanie Spinner. Used by permission of Random House Children's Books, a division of Penguin Random House LLC; page 90: "Letters to My Daughter #3" by Judith Minty from *Letters to My Daughter* by Judith Minty. Copyright © 1980 by Judith Minty. Courtesy of Mayapple Press; page 144: Illustration by Lulu Delacre from *Turning Pages: My Life Story* by Sonia Sotomayor. Copyright © 2018 by Lulu Delacre. Used by permission of Philomel, an imprint of Penguin Young Readers Group, a division of Penguin Random House LLC. All rights reserved.

2 3 4 5 6 7 8 9 10   40   29 28 27 26 25 24 23 22 21

Scholastic Inc., 557 Broadway, New York, NY 10012